MW01233357

ACLS

Success

By Lewis Morris

Copyright © Network4Learning, Inc.

2018.

www.insiderswords.com/ACLS

ISBN-13: 978-1983272127

Table of Contents

What is "Insider Language"?

Recent research has confirmed what we have known for decades: The strongest students and leaders in industry have a mastered an Insider Language in their subject and field. This Insider language is made up of the technical terms and vocabulary necessary to communicate effectively in classes or the workplace. For those who master it, learning is easier, faster, and much more enjoyable.

Most students who are surveyed report that the greatest challenge to any course of study is learning the vocabulary. When we examine typical college courses, we discover that there is, on average, 250 Insider Terms a student must learn over the course of a semester. Further, most exams rely heavily on this set of words for assessment purposes. The structure of multiple choice exams lends itself perfectly to the testing of this Insider Language. Students who can differentiate between Insider Language terms can handle challenging exam questions with ease and confidence.

From recent research on learning and vocabulary we have learned:

- Your knowledge of any subject is contained in the content-specific words you know. The more of these terms that you know, the easier it is to understand and recall important information; the easier it will be to communicate your ideas to peers, professors, supervisors, and co-workers. The stronger your content-area vocabulary is, the higher your scores will be on your exams and written assignments.

- Students who develop a strong Insider Language perform better on tests, learn faster, retain more information, and express greater satisfaction in learning.

- Familiarizing yourself with subject-area vocabulary before formal study (pre-learning) is the most effective way to learn this language and reap the most benefit.

- The vocabulary on standardized exams come directly from the stated objectives of the test-makers. This means that the vocabulary found on standardized exams is predictable. Our books focus on this vocabulary.

- Most multiple-choice exams are glorified vocabulary quizzes. Think about the format of a multiple-choice question. The question stem is a definition of a term and the choices (known as distractors) are 4 or 5 similar words. Your task is to differentiate between the meanings of those terms and choose the correct word.

- It takes a person several exposures to a new word to be able to use it with confidence in conversation or in writing. You need to process these words several different ways to make them part of your long-term memory.

The goals of this book are:

- To give you an "Insider Language" for your subject.
- Pre-teach the most important words before you set out on a traditional course of review or study.
- Teach you the most important words in your subject area.
- Teach you strategies for learning subject-area words on your own.
- Boost your confidence in your ability to master this language and support you in your study.
- Reduce the stress of studying and provide you with fun activities that work.

How it works:

The secret to mastering Insider Language is through repetition and exposure. We have eleven steps for you to follow:

1. Read the word and definition in the glossary out loud. "See it, Say it"
2. Identify the part of speech the word belongs to such as noun, verb, adverb, or adjective. This will help you group the word and identify similar words.
3. Place the word in context by using it in a sentence. Write this sentence down and read it aloud.
4. Use "Chunking" to group the words. Make a diagram or word cloud using these groups.
5. Make connections to the words by creating analogies.
6. Create mnemonics that help you recognize patterns and orders of words by substituting the words for more memorable items or actions.
7. Examine the morphology of the word, that is, identify the root, prefix, and suffix that make up the word. Identify similar and related words.
8. Complete word games and puzzles such as crosswords and word searches.
9. Complete matching questions that require you to differentiate between related words.
10. Complete Multiple-choice questions containing the words.
11. Create a visual metaphor or "memory cartoon" to make a mental picture of the word and related processes.

By completing this word study process, you will be exposed to the terminology in various ways that will activate your memory and create a lasting understanding of this language.

The strategies in this book are designed to make you an independent expert at learning insider language. These strategies include:

- Verbalizing the word by reading it and its definition aloud ("See It, Say It"). This allows you to make visual, auditory, and speech connections with its meaning.

- Identifying the type of word (Noun, verb, adverb, and adjective). Making this distinction helps you understand how to visualize the word. It helps you "chunk" the words into groups, and gives you clues on how to use the word.

- Place the word in context by using it in a sentence. Write this sentence down and read it aloud. This will give you an example of how the word is used.

- "Chunking". By breaking down the word list into groups of closely related words, you will learn them better and be able to remember them faster. Once you have group the terms, you can then make word clouds using a free online service. These word clouds provide visual cues to remembering the words and their meanings.

- Analogies. By creating analogies for essential words, you will be making connections that you can see on paper. These connections can trigger your memory and activate your ability to use the word in your writing as you begin to use them. Many of these analogies also use visual cues. In a sense, you can make a mental picture from the analogy.

- Mnemonics. A device such as a pattern of letters, ideas, or associations that assists in remembering something. A mnemonic is especially useful for remembering the order of a set of words or the order of a process.

- Morphology. The study of word roots, prefixes, and suffixes. By examining the structure of the words, you will gain insight into other words that are closely related, and learn how to best use the word.

- Visual metaphors. This is the most sophisticated and entertaining strategy for learning vocabulary. Create a "memory cartoon" using one or more of the vocabulary terms. This activity triggers the visual part of your memory and makes fast, permanent, imprints of the word on your memory. By combining the terms in your visual metaphor, you can "chunk" the entire set of vocabulary terms into several visual metaphors and benefit from the brain's tendency to group these terms.

The activities in this book are designed to imprint the words and their meanings in your memory in different ways. By completing each activity, you will gain the necessary exposures to the word to make it a permanent part of your vocabulary. Each activity uses a different part of your memory. The result is that you will be comfortable using these words and be able to tell the difference between closely related words. The activities include:

A. Crossword Puzzles and Word Searches- These are proven to increase test scores and improve comprehension. Students frequently report that they are fun and engaging, while requiring them to analyze the structure and meaning of the words.

B. Matching- This activity is effective because it forces you to differentiate between many closely related terms.

C. Multiple Choice- This classic question format lends itself to vocabulary study perfectly. Most exams are in this format because they are simple to make, easy to score, and are a reliable type of assessment. (Perfect for the Vocabulary Master!) One strategy to use with multiple choice questions that enhance their effectiveness is to cover the answer choices while you read the question. After reading the question, see if you can answer it before looking at the choices. Then look at the choices to see if you match one of them.

Conducting a thorough "word study" of your insider language will take time and effort, but the rewards will be well worth it. By following this guide and completing the exercises thoughtfully, you will become a stronger, more effective, and satisfied student. Best of luck on your mastery of this Insider Language!

Insider Language Strategies

"See It, Say It!" Reading your Insider Language set aloud

"IT IS BETTER TO FAIL IN ORIGINALITY THAN TO SUCCEED IN IMITATION."
–HERMAN MELVILLE

Reading aloud is the foundation for the development of an Insider Language. It is the single most important thing you can do for vocabulary acquisition. Done correctly, it engages the visual, auditory, and speech centers of the brain and hastens its storage in your long-term memory.

Reading aloud demonstrates the relationship between the printed word and its meaning.

You can read aloud on a higher level than you can initially understand, so reading aloud makes complex ideas more accessible and exposes you to vocabulary and patterns that are not part of your typical speech. Reading aloud helps you understand the complicated text better and makes more challenging text easier to grasp and understand. Reading aloud helps you to develop the "habits of mind" the strongest students use.

Reading aloud will make connections to concepts in the reading that requires you to relate the new vocabulary to things you already know. Go to the glossary at the end of this book and for each word complete the five steps outlined below:

1. Read the word and its definition aloud. Focus on the sound of the word and how it looks on the paper.
2. Read the word aloud again try to say three or four similar words; this will help you build connections to closely related words.
3. Read the word aloud a third time. Try to make a connection to something you have read or heard.
4. Visualize the concept described in the term. Paint a mental picture of the word in use.
5. Try to think of the opposite of the word. Discovering a close antonym will help you place this word in context.

Create a sentence using the word in its proper context

"OPPORTUNITIES DON'T HAPPEN. YOU CREATE THEM." –CHRIS GROSSER

Context means the circumstances that form the setting for an event, statement, or idea, and which it can be fully understood and assessed. Synonyms for context include conditions, factors, situation, background, and setting.
Place the word in context by using it in a sentence. Write this sentence down and read it aloud. By creating sentences, you are practicing using the word correctly. If you strive to make these sentences interesting and creative, they will become more memorable and effective in activating your long-term memory.

Identify the Parts of Speech
"SUCCESS IS NOT FINAL; FAILURE IS NOT FATAL: IT IS THE COURAGE TO CONTINUE THAT COUNTS." –WINSTON S. CHURCHILL

Read through each term in the glossary and make a note of what part of speech each term is. Studying and identifying parts of speech shows us how the words relate to each other. It also helps you create a visualization of each term. Below are brief descriptions of the parts of speech for you to use as a guide.

VERB: A word denoting action, occurrence, or existence. Examples: walk, hop, whisper, sweat, dribbles, feels, sleeps, drink, smile, are, is, was, has.

NOUN: A word that names a person, place, thing, idea, animal, quality, or action. Nouns are the subject of the sentence. Examples: dog, Tom, Florida, CD, pasta, hate, tiger.

ADJECTIVE: A word that modifies, qualifies, or describes nouns and pronouns. Generally, adjectives appear immediately before the words they modify. Examples: smart girl, gifted teacher, old car, red door.

ADVERB: A word that modifies verbs, adjectives and other adverbs. An "ly" ending almost always changes an adjective to an adverb. Examples: ran swiftly, worked slowly, and drifted aimlessly. Many adverbs do not end in "ly." However, all adverbs identify when, where, how, how far, how much, etc. Examples: run hot, lived hard, moved right, study smart.

Chunking

"YOUR POSITIVE ACTION COMBINED WITH POSITIVE THINKING RESULTS IN SUCCESS." SHIV KHERA

Chunking is when you take a set of words and break it down into groups based on a common relationship. Research has shown that our brains learn by chunking information. By grouping your terms, you will be able to recall large sets of these words easily. To help make your chunking go easily use an online word cloud generator to make a set of word clouds representing your chunks.

1. Study the glossary and decide how you want to chunk the set of words. You can group by part of speech, topic, letter of the alphabet, word length, etc. Try to find an easy way to group each term.
2. Once you have your different groups, visit www.wordclouds.com to create a custom word cloud for each group. Print each one of these clouds and post it in a prominent place to serve as constant visual aids for your learning.

Analogies

"CHOOSE THE POSITIVE. YOU HAVE CHOICE, YOU ARE MASTER OF YOUR ATTITUDE, CHOOSE THE POSITIVE, THE CONSTRUCTIVE. OPTIMISM IS A FAITH THAT LEADS TO SUCCESS."– BRUCE LEE

An analogy is a comparison in which an idea or a thing is compared to another thing that is quite different from it. Analogies aim at explaining an idea by comparing it to something that is familiar. Metaphors and similes are tools used to create analogies.

Analogies are useful for learning vocabulary because they require you to analyze a word (or words), and then transfer that analysis to another word. This transfer reinforces the understanding of all the words.

As you analyze the relationships between the analogies you are creating, you will begin to understand the complex relationships between the seemingly unrelated words.

__A__ is to __B_ as __C_ is to __D_

This can be written using colons in place of the terms "is to" and "as."

A:B::C:D

The two items on the left (items A & B) describe a relationship and are separated by a single colon. The two items on the right (items C & D) are shown on the right and are also separated by a colon. Together, both sides are then separated by two colons in the middle, as shown here: Tall: Short :: Skinny: Fat. The relationship used in this analogy is the antonym.

How to create an analogy

Start with the basic formula for an analogy:

_____ : _____ :: _____ : _____

Next, we will examine a simple synonym analogy:

automobile : car :: box : crate

The key to figuring out a set of word analogies is determining the relationship between the paired set of words.

Here is a list of the most common types of Analogies and examples

Synonym	Scream : Yell :: Push : Shove
Antonym	Rich : Poor :: Empty : Full
Cause is to Effect	Prosperity : Happiness :: Success : Joy
A Part is to its Whole	Toe : Foot :: Piece : Set
An Object to its Function	Car : Travel :: Read : Learn
A Item is to its Category	Tabby : House Cat :: Doberman : Dog
Word is a symptom of the other	Pain : Fracture :: Wheezing : Allergy
An object and it's description	Glass : Brittle :: Lead : Dense
The word is lacking the second word	Amputee : Limb :: Deaf : Hearing
The first word Hinders the second word	Shackles : Movement :: Stagger : Walk
The first word helps the action of the second	Knife : Bread :: Screwdriver : Screw
This word is made up of the second word	Sweater : Wool :: Jeans : Denim
A word and it's definition	Cede: Break Away :: Abolish : To get rid of

Using words from the glossary, make a set of analogies using each one. As a bonus, use more than one glossary term in a single analogy.

_____ : _____ :: _____ : _____

Name the relationship between the words in your analogy:_____

_____ : _____ :: _____ : _____

Name the relationship between the words in your analogy:_____

_____ : _____ :: _____ : _____

Name the relationship between the words in your analogy:_____

Mnemonics

"IT ISN'T THE MOUNTAINS AHEAD TO CLIMB THAT WEAR YOU OUT; IT'S THE PEBBLE IN YOUR SHOE."   **–MUHAMMAD ALI**

A mnemonic is a learning technique that helps you retain and remember information. Mnemonics are one of the best learning methods for remembering lists or processes in order. Mnemonics make the material more meaningful by adding associations and creating patterns. Interestingly, mnemonics may work better when they utilize absurd, startling, or shocking examples and references. Mnemonics help organize the information so that you can easily retrieve it later. By giving you associations and cues, mnemonics allow you to form a mental structure ordering a list or process to help you remember it better. This mental structure allows you to create a structure of association between items that may not appear to have any relationship. Mnemonics typically use references that are easy to visualize and thus easier to remember. Through visualization of vivid images and references, the information is much easier to imprint into long-term memory. The power of making mnemonics lies in converting dull, inert and uninspiring information into something vibrant and memorable.

How to make simple and effective mnemonics
Some of the best mnemonics help us remember simple rules or lists in order.

Step 1. Take a list of terms you are trying to remember in order. For example, we will use the scientific method:

> observation, question, hypothesis, methods, results, and conclusion.

Next, we will replace each word on the list with a new word that starts with the same letter. These new words will together form a vivid sentence that is easy to remember:

> Objectionable Queens Haunted Macho Rednecks Creatively.

As silly as the above sentence seems, it is easy to remember, and now we can call on this sentence to remind us of the order of the scientific method.

Visit http://www.mnemonicgenerator.com/ and try typing in a list of words. It is fun to see the mnemonics that it makes and shows how easy it is to make great mnemonics to help your studying.

Using vivid words in your mnemonics allows you to see the sentence you are making. Words that are gross, scary, or name interesting animals are helpful. Profanity is also useful because the shock value can trigger memory. The following are lists of vivid words to use in your mnemonics:

Gross words

Moist, Gurgle, Phlegm, Fetus, Curd, Smear, Squirt, Chunky, Orifice, Maggots, Viscous, Queasy, Bulbous, Pustule, Putrid, Fester, Secrete, Munch, Vomit, Ooze, Dripping, Roaches, Mucus, Stink, Stank, Stunk, Slurp, Pus, Lick, Salty, Tongue, Fart, Flatulence, Hemorrhoid.

Interesting Animals

Aardvark, Baboon, Chicken, Chinchilla, Duck, Dragonfly, Emu, Electric Eel, Frog, Flamingo, Gecko, Hedgehog, Hyena, Iguana, Jackal, Jaguar, Leopard, Lynx, Minnow, Manatee, Mongoose, Neanderthal, Newt, Octopus, Oyster, Pelican, Penguin, Platypus, Quail, Racoon, Rattlesnake, Rhinoceros, Scorpion, Seahorse, Toucan, Turkey, Vulture, Weasel, Woodpecker, Yak, Zebra.

Superhero Words

Diabolical, Activate, Boom, Clutch, Dastardly, Dynamic, Dynamite, Shazam, Kaboom, Zip, Zap, Zoom, Zany, Crushing, Smashing, Exploding, Ripping, Tearing.

Scary Words

Apparition, Bat, Chill, Demon, Eerie, Fangs, Genie, Hell, Lantern, Macabre, Nightmare, Owl, Ogre, Phantasm, Repulsive, Scarecrow, Tarantula, Undead, Vampire, Wraith, Zombie.

There are several types of mnemonics that can help your memory.

1. Images

Visual mnemonics are a type of mnemonic that works by associating an image with characters or objects whose name sounds like the item that must be memorized. This is one of the easiest ways to create effective mnemonics. An example would be to use the shape of numbers to help memorize a long list of them. Numbers can be memorized by their shapes, so that: 0 -looks like an egg; 1 -a pencil, or a candle; 2 -a snake; 3 -an ear; 4 -a sailboat; 5 -a key; 6 -a comet; 7 -a knee; 8 -a snowman; 9 -a comma.

Another type of visual mnemonic is the word-length mnemonic in which the number of letters in each word corresponds to a digit. This simple mnemonic gives pi to seven decimal places:

3.141582 becomes "How I wish I could calculate pi."

Of course, you could use this type of mnemonic to create a longer sentence showing the digits of an important number. Some people have used this type of mnemonic to memorize thousands of digits.

Using the hands is also an important tool for creating visual objects. Making the hands into specific shapes can help us remember the pattern of things or the order of a list of things.

2. Rhyming

Rhyming mnemonics are quick ways to make things memorable. A classic example is a mnemonic for the number of days in each month:
"30 days hath September, April, June, and November.
All the rest have 31
Except February, my dear son.
It has 28, and that is fine
But in Leap Year it has 29."

Another example of a rhyming mnemonic is a common spelling rule:
"I before e except after c
or when sounding like a
in neighbor and weigh."

Use **rhymer.com** to get large lists of rhyming words.

3. Homonym

A homonym is one of a group of words that share the same pronunciation but have different meanings, whether spelled the same or not.

Try saying what you're attempting to remember out loud or very quickly, and see if anything leaps out. If you know other languages, using similar-sounding words from those can be effective.

You could also browse this list of homonyms
at http://www.cooper.com/alan/homonym_list.html.

4. Onomatopoeia

An Onomatopeia is a word that phonetically imitates, resembles or suggests the source of the sound that it describes. Are there any noises made by the thing you're trying to memorize? Is it often associated with some other sound? Failing that, just make up a noise that seems to fit.

Achoo, ahem, baa, bam, bark, beep, beep beep, belch, bleat, boo, boo hoo, boom, burp, buzz, chirp, click clack, crash, croak, crunch, cuckoo, dash, drip, ding dong, eek, fizz, flit, flutter, gasp, grrr, ha ha, hee hee, hiccup, hiss, hissing, honk, icky, itchy, jiggly, jangle, knock knock, lush, la la la, mash, meow, moan, murmur, neigh, oink, ouch, plop, pow, quack, quick, rapping, rattle, ribbit, roar, rumble, rustle, scratch, sizzle, skittering, snap crackle pop, splash, splish splash, spurt, swish, swoosh, tap, tapping, tick tock, tinkle, tweet, ugh, vroom, wham, whinny, whip, whooping, woof.

5. Acronyms

An acronym is a word or name formed as an abbreviation from the initial components of a word, such as NATO, which stands for North Atlantic Treaty Organization. If you're trying to memorize something involving letters, this is often a good bet. A lot of famous mnemonics are acronyms, such as ROYGBIV which stands for the order of colors in the light spectrum (Red, Orange, Yellow, Green, Blue, Indigo, and Violet).

A great acronym generator to try is: www.all-acronyms.com.

A different spin on an acronym is a backronym. A **backronym** is a specially constructed phrase that is supposed to be the source of a word that is an acronym. A backronym is constructed by creating a new phrase to fit an already existing word, name, or acronym.

The word is a combination of *backward* and *acronym*, and has been defined as a "reverse acronym." For example, the United States Department of Justice assigns to their Amber Alert program the meaning "**A**merica's **M**issing: **B**roadcast **E**mergency **R**esponse." The process can go either way to make good mnemonics.

Visit: https://arthurdick.com/projects/backronym/ to try out a simple backronym generator.

6. Anagrams

An anagram is a direct word switch or word play, the result of rearranging the letters of a word or phrase to produce a new word or phrase, using all the original letters exactly once; for example, the word anagram can be rearranged into nag-a-ram.

Try re-arranging letters or components and see if anything memorable emerges. Visit http://www.nameacronym.net/ to use a simple anagram generator.

One particularly memorable form of anagram is the spoonerism, where you swap the initial syllables or letters of words to make new phrases. These are usually humorous, and this makes them easier to remember. Here are some examples:

"Is it kisstomary to cuss the bride?" (as opposed to "customary to kiss")
"The Lord is a shoving leopard." (instead of "a loving shepherd")
"A blushing crow." ("crushing blow")
"A well-boiled icicle" ("well-oiled bicycle")
"You were fighting a liar in the quadrangle." ("lighting a fire")
"Is the bean dizzy?" (as opposed to "is the dean busy?")

7. Stories

Make up quick stories or incidents involving the material you want to memorize. For larger chunks of information, the stories can get more elaborate. Structured stories are particularly good for remembering lists or other sequenced information. Have a look at https://en.wikipedia.org/wiki/Method_of_loci for a more advanced memory sequencing technique.

Visual Metaphors

"LIMITS, LIKE FEAR, IS OFTEN AN ILLUSION." –MICHAEL JORDAN

What is a Metaphor?

A metaphor is a figure of speech that refers to one thing by mentioning another thing. Metaphors provide clarity and identify hidden similarities between two seemingly unrelated ideas. A visual metaphor is an image that creates a link between different ideas.

Visual metaphors help us use our understanding of the world to learn new concepts, skills, and ideas. Visual metaphors help us relate new material to what we already know. Visual metaphors must be clear and simple enough to spark a connection and understanding. Visual metaphors should use familiar things to help you be less fearful of new, complex, or challenging topics. Metaphors trigger a sense of familiarity so that you are more accepting of the new idea. Metaphors work best when you associate a familiar, easy to understand idea with a challenging, obscure, or abstract concept.

How to make a visual metaphor

1. Brainstorm using the words of the concept. Use different fonts, colors, or shapes to represent parts of the concept.

2. Merge these images together

3. Show the process using arrows, accents, etc.

4. Think about the story line your metaphor projects.

Examples of visual metaphors:

A skeleton used to show a framework of something.

A cloud showing an outline.

A bodybuilder whose muscles represent supporting ideas and details.

A sandwich where the meat, tomato, and lettuce represent supporting ideas.

A recipe card to show a process.

Your metaphor should be accurate. It should be complex enough to convey meaning, but simple and clear enough to be easily understood.

Morphology
"SCIENCE IS THE CAPTAIN, AND PRACTICE THE SOLDIERS." LEONARDO DA VINCI

Morphology is the study of the origin, roots, suffixes, and prefixes of the words. Understanding the meaning of prefixes, suffixes, and roots make it easier to decode the meaning of new vocabulary. Having the ability to decode using morphology increases text comprehension when initially reading as well.

The capability of identifying meaningful parts of words (morphemes), including prefixes, suffixes, and roots can be helpful. Identifying morphemes improves decoding accuracy and fluency. Reading speed improves when you can decode larger chunks of text quickly. When you can recognize morphemes in words, you will be better able to make sense of new words in context. Below are charts containing the most common prefixes, suffixes, and root words. Use them to help you decode your vocabulary terms.

Prefixes

Prefix	Meaning	Example words and meanings	
a, ab, abs	away from	absent abdicate	not to be present, to give up an office or throne.
ad, a, ac, af, ag, an, ar, at, as	to, toward	Advance advantage	To move forward To have the upper hand
anti	against	Antidote antisocial antibiotic	To repair poisoning refers to someone who's not social
bi, bis	two	bicycle binary biweekly	two-wheeled cycle two number system every two weeks
circum, cir	around	circumnavigate circle	Travel around the world a figure that goes all around
com, con, co, col	with, together	Complete Complement	To finish To go along with
de	away from, down, the opposite of	depart detour	to go away from to go out of your way
dis, dif, di	apart	dislike dishonest distant	not to like not honest away
En-, em-	Cause to	Entrance	the way in.
epi	upon, on top of	epitaph epilogue epidemic	writing upon a tombstone speech at the end, on top of the rest
equ, equi	equal	equalize equitable	to make equal fair, equal
ex, e, ef	out, from	exit eject exhale	to go out to throw out to breathe out
Fore-	Before	Forewarned	To have prior warning

Prefix	Meaning	Example Words and Meanings	
in, il, ir, im, en	in, into	Infield Imbibe	The inner playing field to take part in
in, il, ig, ir, im	not	inactive ignorant irreversible irritate	not active not knowing not reversible to put into discomfort
inter	between, among	international interact	among nations to mix with
mal, male	bad, ill, wrong	malpractice malfunction	bad practice fail to function, bad function
Mid	Middle	Amidships	In the middle of a ship
mis	wrong, badly	misnomer	The wrong name
mono	one, alone, single	monocle	one lensed glasses
non	not, the reverse of	nonprofit	not making a profit
ob	in front, against, in front of, in the way of	Obsolete	No longer needed
omni	everywhere, all	omnipresent omnipotent	always present, everywhere all powerful
Over	On top	Overdose	Take too much medication
Pre	Before	Preview	Happens before a show.
per	through	Permeable pervasive	to pass through, all encompassing
poly	many	Polygamy polygon	many spouses figure with many sides
post	after	postpone postmortem	to do after after death
pre	before, earlier than	Predict Preview	To know before To view before release
pro	forward, going ahead of, supporting	proceed pro-war promote	to go forward supporting the war to raise or move forward
re	again, back	retell recall reverse	to tell again to call back to go back
se	apart	secede seclude	to withdraw, become apart to stay apart from others
Semi	Half	Semipermeable	Half-permeable

Prefix	Meaning	Example Words and Meanings	
Sub	under, less than	Submarine	under water
super	over, above, greater	superstar superimpose	a start greater than her stars to put over something else
trans	across	transcontinental transverse	across the continent to lie or go across
un, uni	one	unidirectional unanimous unilateral	having one direction sharing one view having one side
un	not	uninterested unhelpful unethical	not interested not helpful not ethical

Roots

Root	Meaning	Example words & meanings	
act, ag	to do, to act	Agent Activity	One who acts as a representative Action
Aqua	Water	Aquamarine	The color of water
Aud	To hear	Auditorium	A place to hear music
apert	open	Aperture	An opening
bas	low	Basement Basement	Something that is low, at the bottom A room that is low
Bio	Living thing	Biological	Living matter
cap, capt, cip, cept, ceive	to take, to hold, to seize	Captive Receive Capable Recipient	One who is held To take Able to take hold of things One who takes hold or receives
ced, cede, ceed, cess	to go, to give in	Precede Access Proceed	To go before Means of going to To go forward
Cogn	Know	Cognitive	Ability to think
cred, credit	to believe	Credible Incredible Credit	Believable Not believable Belief, trust
curr, curs, cours	to run	Current Precursory Recourse	Now in progress, running Running (going) before To run for aid
Cycle	Circle	Lifecycle	The circle of life
dic, dict	to say	Dictionary Indict	A book explaining words (sayings)

Root	Meaning	Examples and meanings	
duc, duct	to lead	Induce Conduct Aqueduct	To lead to action To lead or guide Pipe that leads water somewhere
equ	equal, even	Equality Equanimity	Equal in social, political rights Evenness of mind, tranquility
fac, fact, fic, fect, fy	to make, to do	Facile Fiction Factory Affect	Easy to do Something that is made up Place that makes things To make a change in
fer, ferr	to carry, bring	Defer Referral	To carry away Bring a source for help/information
Gen	Birth	Generate	To create something
graph	write	Monograph Graphite	A writing on a particular subject A form of carbon used for writing
Loc	Place	Location	A place
Mater	Mother	Maternity	Expecting birth
Mem	Recall	Memory	The recall experiences
mit, mis	to send	Admit Missile	To send in Something sent through the air
Nat	Born	Native	Born in a place
par	equal	Parity Disparate	Equality No equal, not alike
Ped	Foot	Podiatrist	Foot doctor
Photo	Light	Photograph	A picture
plic	to fold, to bend, to turn	Complicate Implicate	To fold (mix) together To fold in, to involve
pon, pos, posit, pose	to place	Component Transpose Compose Deposit	A part placed together with others A place across To put many parts into place To place for safekeeping
scrib, script	to write	Describe Transcript Subscription	To write about or tell about A written copy A written signature or document
sequ, secu	to follow	Sequence	In following order

Root	Meaning	Examples and Meanings	
Sign	Mark	Signal	to alert somebody
spec, spect, spic	to appear, to look, to see	Specimen Aspect	An example to look at One way to see something
sta, stat, sist,	to stand, or make stand	Constant	Standing with
stit, sisto	Stable, steady	Status Stable Desist	Social standing Steady (standing) To stand away from
Struct	To build	Construction	To build a thing
tact	to touch	Contact Tactile	To touch together To be able to be touched
ten, tent, tain	to hold	Tenable Retentive Maintain	Able to be held, holding Holding To keep or hold up
tend, tens, tent	to stretch	Extend Tension	To stretch or draw out Stretched
Therm	Temperature	Thermometer	Detects temperature
tract	to draw	Attract Contract	To draw together An agreement drawn up
ven, vent	to come	Convene Advent	To come together A coming
Vis	See	Invisible	Cannot be seen
ver, vert, vers	to turn	Avert Revert Reverse	To turn away To turn back To turn around

Crossword Puzzles

1. *Using the Across and Down clues, write the correct words in the numbered grid below.*

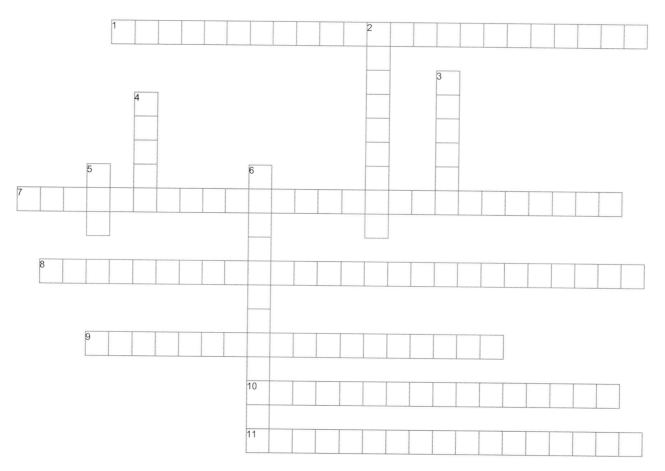

ACROSS

1. A congenital heart defect where an abnormal opening in the septum separates the ventricles.
7. A genetic disorder of the heart in which the heart muscle becomes abnormally thick, making it harder to pump blood.
8. A condition in which the left ventricle of the heart exhibits decreased functionality. This can lead to heart failure.
9. Death as a result of sudden cardiac arrest.
10. Large vein that carries deoxygenated blood from the lower venous circulation (below the neck) and empties into the Right Atrium.
11. A normal heart rate.

DOWN

2. A cluster of cells in the upper right atrium that generates electrical impulses and stimulates the heart to contract and pump blood.
3. The upper chamber of each half of the heart.
4. A tube designed to be implanted in a vessel to help keep it open.
5. A life-saving device that treats sudden cardiac arrest.
6. A rapid twitching of the heart muscles caused by an abnormal and sometimes chaotic discharge of electrical impulses. Atrial fibrillation results in a rapid and irregular heartbeat.

A. Sinus Node
D. Atrium
G. Normal Sinus Rhythm
J. Stent

B. Fibrillation
E. AED
H. Ventricular Septal Defect
K. Hypertrophic Cardiomyopathy

C. Left Ventricular Dysfunction
F. Sudden Cardiac Death
I. Inferior Vena Cava

© 2017 Network4Learning, Inc.

2. *Using the Across and Down clues, write the correct words in the numbered grid below.*

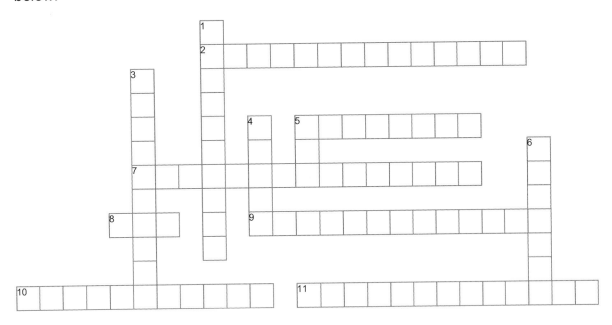

ACROSS

2. Return of membrane potential to its resting state. K+ move into the cell and Na+ moves out.

5. A thin, flexible tube that is inserted into the heart through a peripheral blood vessel to provide therapy and

7. Meets criteria for NSR except rhythm is irregular.

8. Coronary artery that supplies oxygenated blood to the anterior surface of the left ventricle, the ventricular septum, and the papillary muscles of the mitral valve and the bundle of His.

9. An unusually large heart. This condition can be a a result of conditions such as an abnormal heart rhythm, stress, or weakening of the heart muscle.

10. Conducts impulses from AV node to bundle branches; makes up AV junction

11. High pressure chamber of the heart responsible for pumping oxygenated blood to the systemic circulation.

DOWN

1. Smooth ridges on the walls of the heart.

3. Pause caused by delay in impulse being initiated in the SA node. pause is < 2 R-R intervals.

4. The first negative deflection following the P wave.

5. cardiopulmonary resuscitation.

6. A PVC that falls on or very near the T wave.

A. Sinus Arrhythmia
E. Bundle of His
I. Sinus Pause

B. R ON T PVC
F. Catheter
J. Left Ventricle

C. Trabeculae
G. Enlarged Heart
K. LAD

D. CPR
H. Repolarization
L. Q wave

© 2017 Network4Learning, Inc.

3. *Using the Across and Down clues, write the correct words in the numbered grid below.*

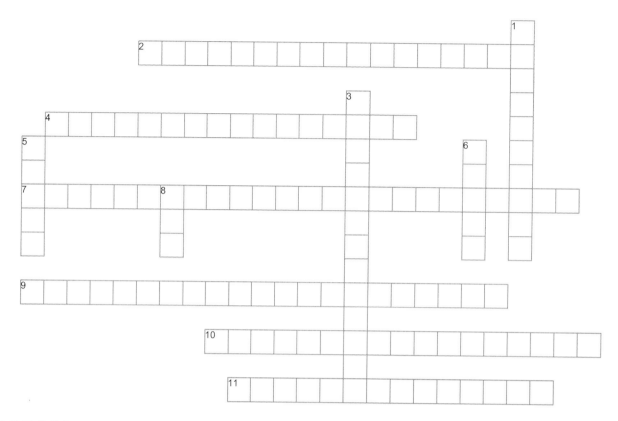

ACROSS

2. Caused by stimulation of para-sympathetic Nervous System and results in slowing of the Heart Rate. Can be initiated intentionally with carotid massage or valsalva maneuver.

4. Fundamental treatment provided to a victim to include CPR and AED use.

7. A non-profit organization that establishes the standards in cardiac care.

9. Originates in the ventricle. Rate is 20-40bpm.

10. A rapid heart rhythm resulting in 160-190 beats per minute and is a type of supraventricular tachycardia.

11. Final part of the conduction system that initiates vent. depolarization.

DOWN

1. The upper left chamber of the heart that receives oxygenated blood from the lungs and pumps it to the left ventricle.

3. Immunity protection provided by each state government and the Federal government to encourage lay responders to treat a victim of sudden cardiac arrest with an AED and CPR.

5. Part of the ECG complex that reflects atrial depolarization.

6. Ventricular repolarization; follows the QRS complex.

8. A life-saving device that treats sudden cardiac arrest.

A. P Wave
D. Vasovagal Response
G. Basic Life Support
J. Left Atrium

B. American Heart Association
E. Idioventricular Rhythm
H. Purkinje Fibers
K. T wave

C. AED
F. Good Samaritan
I. Atrial Tachycardia

© 2017 Network4Learning, Inc.

4. *Using the Across and Down clues, write the correct words in the numbered grid below.*

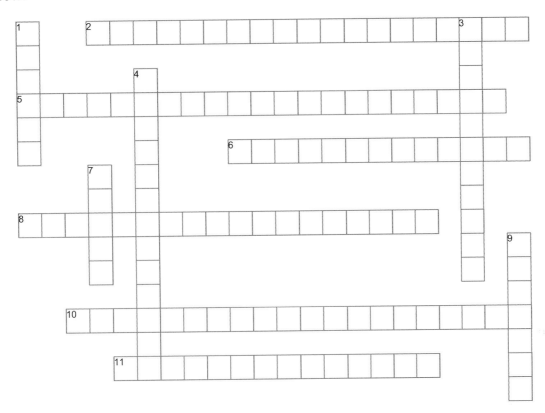

ACROSS

2. An advanced life support medical device that monitors the heart rhythm and allow the user to manually set the energy delivery and deliver a shock.

5. Originates in the ventricle. Rate is 20-40bpm.

6. High pressure chamber of the heart responsible for pumping oxygenated blood to the systemic circulation.

8. A four-step process for treating victims of sudden cardiac arrest.

10. Complex or rhythm that takes over if SA node fails. Beats or rhythm occur after a pause and later than expected.

11. The act of using equipment to send an electrical shock to the heart to stop an irregular heart rhythm. Defibrillation is the only cure to sudden cardiac arrest.

DOWN

1. The upper chamber of each half of the heart.

3. A rapid heart rate, usually over 100 beats per minute.

4. The lower left chamber of the heart that receives oxygenated blood from the left atrium and pumps the blood through the aorta to the body.

7. The 1st positive deflection following the P wave.

9. A rapid, but organized vibration of the heart muscle. Atrial flutter can result in 250-350 heart beats per minute.

A. Chain of Survival
D. Idioventricular Rhythm
G. Left Ventricle
J. R wave

B. Junctional Escape Beat
E. Left Ventricle
H. Flutter
K. Manual Defibrillator

C. Atrium
F. Defibrillation
I. Tachycardia

© 2017 Network4Learning, Inc.

5. *Using the Across and Down clues, write the correct words in the numbered grid below.*

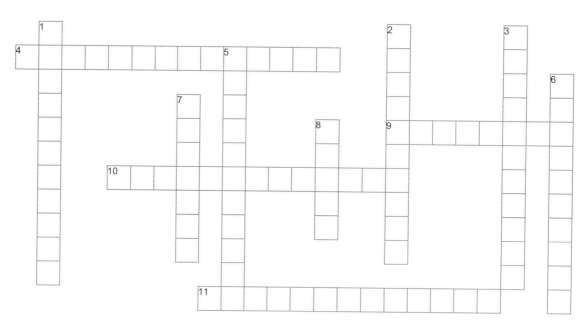

ACROSS

4. One-way valve that allow blood flow from Right Atrium to Right Ventricle.

9. A technique to remove or render inactive problematic cardiac tissue.

10. A medical device used to treat a victim with a life-threatening irregular heart rhythm.

11. An unusually large heart. This condition can be a a result of conditions such as an abnormal heart rhythm, stress, or weakening of the heart muscle.

DOWN

1. The amount of time it takes for ventricle depolarization. Measured from when the QRS first leaves the isoelectric line to where the ST segment begins.

2. Low pressure chamber that receives oxygenated blood from the pulmonary system via the pulmonary veins.

3. Rapid, fluttering heart beats. Heart palpitations can be triggered by exercise, medications, or stress.

5. Alternate with epinephrine in patient with pulseless VFib

6. Pause caused by delay in impulse being initiated in the SA node. pause is < 2 R-R intervals.

7. A heart block where the PR interval becomes progressively longer until the P wave is not conducted through the ventricle and a QRS complex is dropped.

8. Part of the ECG complex that reflects atrial depolarization.

A. Vasopressin
E. Palpitation
I. Enlarged Heart

B. Tricuspid Valve
F. Mobitz I
J. Ablation

C. Sinus Pause
G. QRS Duration
K. Left Atrium

D. Defibrillator
H. P Wave

6. *Using the Across and Down clues, write the correct words in the numbered grid below.*

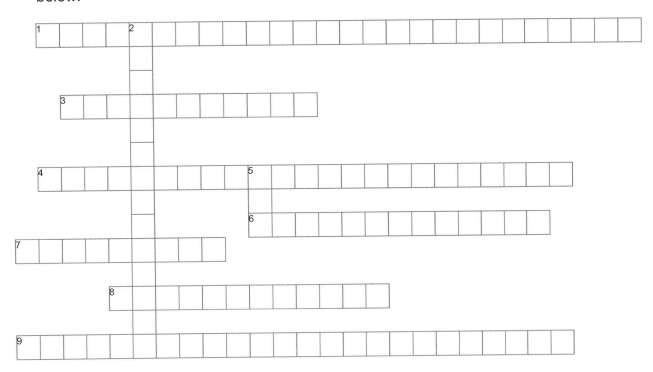

ACROSS

1. A genetic disorder of the heart in which the heart muscle becomes abnormally thick, making it harder to pump blood.

3. Alternate with epinephrine in patient with pulseless VFib

4. Weak disorganized quivering of the ventricle with no identifying QRS complex.

6. A medical device used to treat a victim with a life-threatening irregular heart rhythm.

7. An implantable medical device that sends electrical signals to the heart to set the heart rhythm.

8. A rapid twitching of the heart muscles caused by an abnormal and sometimes chaotic discharge of electrical impulses. Atrial fibrillation results in a rapid and irregular heartbeat.

9. A medical device that is implanted in the body to diagnose and treat abnormal electrical arrhythmias. If an abnormal arrhythmia is detected, the ICD will apply a shock to restore the heart to a normal rhythm.

DOWN

2. Return of membrane potential to its resting state. K+ move into the cell and Na+ moves out.

5. A life-saving device that treats sudden cardiac arrest.

A. Fibrillation
B. Defibrillator
C. Repolarization
D. Ventricular Fibrillation
E. Vasopressin
F. Hypertrophic Cardiomyopathy
G. Implantable Defibrillator
H. Pacemaker
I. AED

© 2017 Network4Learning, Inc.

7. *Using the Across and Down clues, write the correct words in the numbered grid below.*

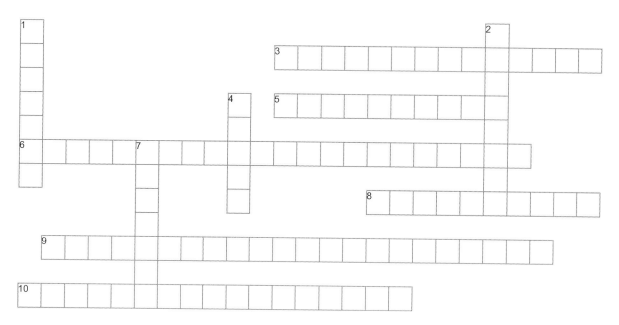

ACROSS

3. A disruption of the heart rhythm caused by a sudden blunt blow to the chest.

5. An abnormality or irregularity in the heart rhythm.

6. Impulse for ventricular contraction originated from ventricle with a rate of > 100pbm.

8. Measured from where the P-wave starts to where the QRS first leaves the isoelectric line. Represents atrial depolarization and the delay in the AV node.

9. A fast heart rhythm that originates in the ventricles. Also known as V-tach.

10. A normal heart rate.

DOWN

1. A PVC that falls on or very near the T wave.

2. Sympathomimetic agent that causes peripheral vasoconstriction (alpha effects) and muscle vasodilation (beta effects).

4. The first negative deflection following the P wave.

7. Used for heart block and ventricular arrhythmias. A sympathomimetic that results in pronounced stimulation of beta1 & beta2 receptors of heart and bronchi.

A. PR interval
D. Ventricular Tachycardia
G. Arrhythmia
J. Q wave

B. Commotio Cordis
E. Ventricular Tachycardia
H. R ON T PVC

C. Normal Sinus Rhythm
F. Isuprel
I. Dopamine

© 2017 Network4Learning, Inc.

8. *Using the Across and Down clues, write the correct words in the numbered grid below.*

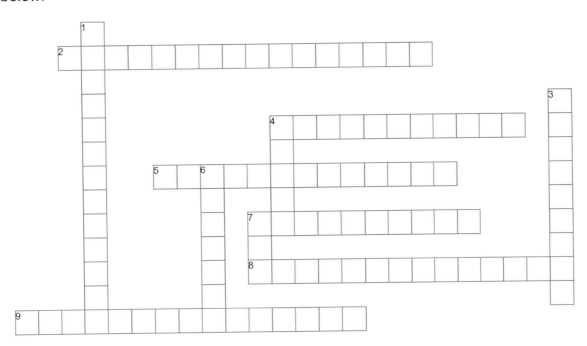

ACROSS

2. Treats Torsades de Pointes, Ventricular Fibrillation. Electrolyte that causes all muscles to contract. Results in depression early after depolarization.

4. The amount of time it takes for ventricle depolarization. Measured from when the QRS first leaves the isoelectric line to where the ST segment begins.

5. Venous drainage system of the heart. Returns de-oxygenated blood from the heart to the Right Atrium.

7. The upper left chamber of the heart that receives oxygenated blood from the lungs and pumps it to the left ventricle.

8. The act of using equipment to send an electrical shock to the heart to stop an irregular heart rhythm. Defibrillation is the only cure to sudden cardiac arrest.

9. Increases force of muscle contraction.

DOWN

1. The amount of blood ejected by the heart in one minute in liters

3. Premature ventricular contractions occurring every third beat.

4. The first negative deflection following the P wave.

6. A PVC that falls on or very near the T wave.

7. Coronary artery that supplies oxygenated blood to the anterior surface of the left ventricle, the ventricular septum, and the papillary muscles of the mitral valve and the bundle of His.

A. Left Atrium
E. QRS Duration
I. Defibrillation

B. Coronary Sinus
F. Inotropic Effect
J. Cardiac Output

C. LAD
G. Trigeminy
K. Magnesium sulfate

D. Q wave
H. R ON T PVC

© 2017 Network4Learning, Inc.

9. *Using the Across and Down clues, write the correct words in the numbered grid below.*

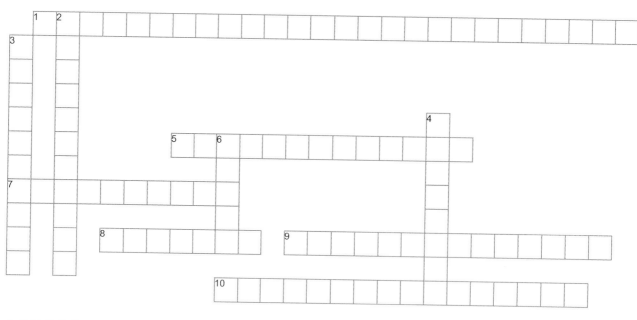

ACROSS

1. An ECG complex that appears earlier than expected; originates from ectopic focus in atrium.

5. The normal rate for a given pacemaker cells.

7. An abnormality or irregularity in the heart rhythm.

8. A rapid, but organized vibration of the heart muscle. Atrial flutter can result in 250-350 heart beats per minute.

9. Current from a defibrillator is delivered two ways. Biphasic therapy was introduced in the 1990s and lowers the electrical threshold for successful defibrillation.

10. Large vein that carries deoxygenated blood from the lower venous circulation (below the neck) and empties into the Right Atrium.

DOWN

2. Low pressure cardiac chamber that receives deoxygenated blood from the systemic venous circulation via the inferior vena cava and the superior vena cava.

3. Pause caused by delay in impulse being initiated in the SA node. pause is < 2 R-R intervals.

4. Para-sympatholytic that blocks acetylcholine effects on post cholinergic receptors in smooth muscle and SA -AV nodes.

6. Ventricular repolarization; follows the QRS complex.

A. Arrhythmia
D. T wave
G. Sinus Pause
J. Biphasic Energy

B. Atropine
E. Right Atrium
H. Inferior Vena Cava

C. Flutter
F. Premature Atrial Contraction
I. Intrinsic Rate

© 2017 Network4Learning, Inc.

10. *Using the Across and Down clues, write the correct words in the numbered grid below.*

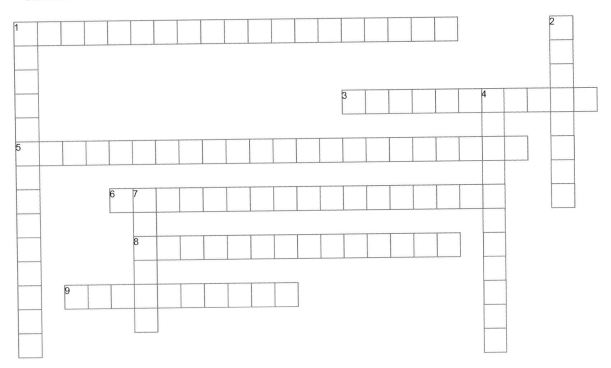

ACROSS

1. Coronary artery that delivers blood to the Right Ventricle, AV junction, and the SA node in 55% of the population.

3. Alternate with epinephrine in patient with pulseless VFib

5. A fast heart rhythm that originates in the ventricles. Also known as V-tach.

6. Caused by stimulation of para-sympathetic Nervous System and results in slowing of the Heart Rate. Can be initiated intentionally with carotid massage or valsalva maneuver.

8. Return of membrane potential to its resting state. K+ move into the cell and Na+ moves out.

9. Pause caused by delay in impulse being initiated in the SA node. pause is < 2 R-R intervals.

DOWN

1. Low pressure cardiac chamber that receives blood from the Right Atrium and pumps it into the pulmonary artery.

2. A heart block where some P waves not conducted through AV node. Some P waves not followed by QRS complexes. P waves that do follow QRS, have consistent intervals.

4. Sympathomimetic that stimulates alpha, beta 1&2 receptors resulting in cardiac stimulation.

7. The upper chamber of each half of the heart.

A. Atrium
D. Sinus Pause
G. Repolarization
J. Right Coronary Artery

B. Mobitz II
E. Epinephrine
H. Vasopressin

C. Ventricular Tachycardia
F. Right Ventricle
I. Vasovagal Response

© 2017 Network4Learning, Inc.

11. *Using the Across and Down clues, write the correct words in the numbered grid below.*

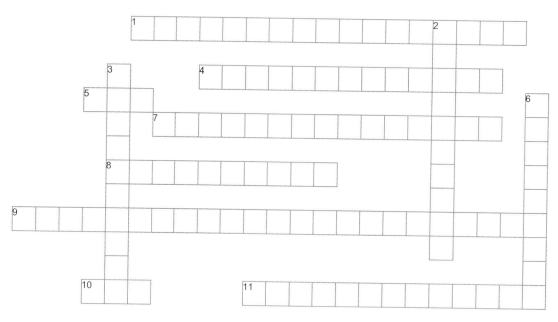

ACROSS

1. Rhythms initiated from impulses that originate from the Atrial Ventricular junction. Intrinsic rate 40-60bpm.

4. An unusually large heart. This condition can be a a result of conditions such as an abnormal heart rhythm, stress, or weakening of the heart muscle.

5. A life-saving device that treats sudden cardiac arrest.

7. Increases force of muscle contraction.

8. An abnormality or irregularity in the heart rhythm.

9. The most common form of sudden cardiac arrest. A sudden, lethal arrhythmia in which chaotic electrical activity results in the ventricles fluttering rapidly and losing the ability to pump blood.

10. A trained and certified professional who can use advanced life support techniques to treat sudden cardiac arrest.

11. High pressure chamber of the heart responsible for pumping oxygenated blood to the systemic circulation.

DOWN

2. Smooth ridges on the walls of the heart.

3. Low pressure chamber that receives oxygenated blood from the pulmonary system via the pulmonary veins.

6. A cluster of cells in the upper right atrium that generates electrical impulses and stimulates the heart to contract and pump blood.

A. AED
D. Junctional Rhythms
G. EMT
J. Arrhythmia

B. Left Atrium
E. Inotropic Effect
H. Trabeculae
K. Enlarged Heart

C. Sinus Node
F. Ventricular Fibrillation
I. Left Ventricle

© 2017 Network4Learning, Inc.

12. *Using the Across and Down clues, write the correct words in the numbered grid below.*

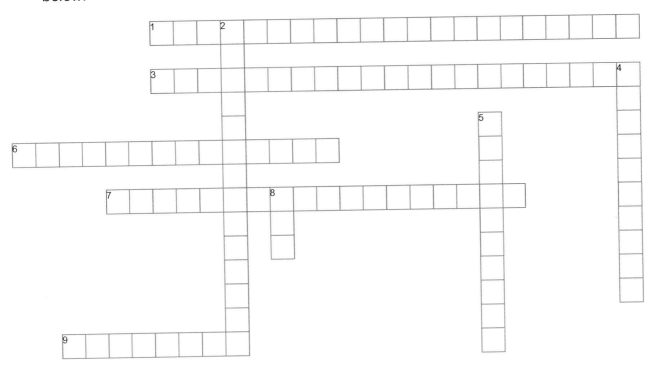

ACROSS

1. Independent activity of atria and ventricles
3. A birth defect of the heart
6. One-way valve that allow blood flow from Right Atrium to Right Ventricle.
7. Death as a result of sudden cardiac arrest.
9. Sympathomimetic agent that causes peripheral vasoconstriction (alpha effects) and muscle vasodilation (beta effects).

DOWN

2. The lower right chamber of the heart that receives deoxygenated blood from the right atrium and pumps it to the lungs through the pulmonary artery.
4. Smooth ridges on the walls of the heart.
5. Low pressure chamber that receives oxygenated blood from the pulmonary system via the pulmonary veins.
8. A life-saving device that treats sudden cardiac arrest.

A. Right Ventricle
D. Trabeculae
G. Tricuspid Valve

B. Congenital Heart Defect
E. Left Atrium
H. Sudden Cardiac Death

C. Third degree Heart Block
F. Dopamine
I. AED

© 2017 Network4Learning, Inc.

13. *Using the Across and Down clues, write the correct words in the numbered grid below.*

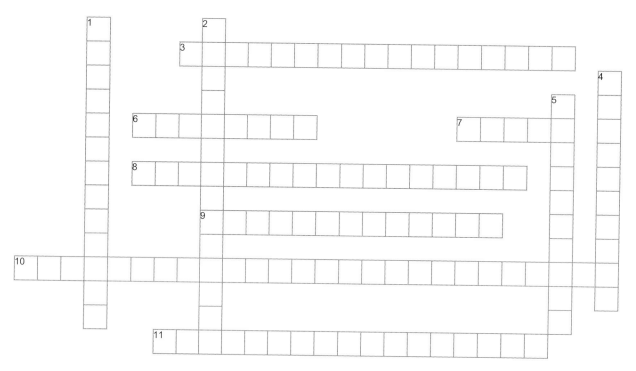

ACROSS

3. polymorphic ventricular tachycardia characterized by QRS complexes that change directions.

6. Para-sympatholytic that blocks acetylcholine effects on post cholinergic receptors in smooth muscle and SA -AV nodes.

7. Part of the ECG complex that reflects atrial depolarization.

8. A rapid heart rhythm resulting in 160-190 beats per minute and is a type of supraventricular tachycardia.

9. Venous drainage system of the heart. Returns de-oxygenated blood from the heart to the Right Atrium.

10. A condition in which the left ventricle of the heart exhibits decreased functionality. This can lead to heart failure.

11. Caused by stimulation of para-sympathetic Nervous System and results in slowing of the Heart Rate. Can be initiated intentionally with carotid massage or valsalva maneuver.

DOWN

1. Immunity protection provided by each state government and the Federal government to encourage lay responders to treat a victim of sudden cardiac arrest with an AED and CPR.

2. A disruption of the heart rhythm caused by a sudden blunt blow to the chest.

4. Anti-arrhythmic used to treat atrial-ventricular tachyarrhythmias.

5. Low pressure chamber that receives oxygenated blood from the pulmonary system via the pulmonary veins.

A. Good Samaritan
D. Commotio Cordis
G. Coronary Sinus
J. P Wave

B. Left Atrium
E. Torsades de Pointes
H. Atrial Tachycardia
K. Atropine

C. Left Ventricular Dysfunction
F. Amiodarone
I. Vasovagal Response

© 2017 Network4Learning, Inc.

14. *Using the Across and Down clues, write the correct words in the numbered grid below.*

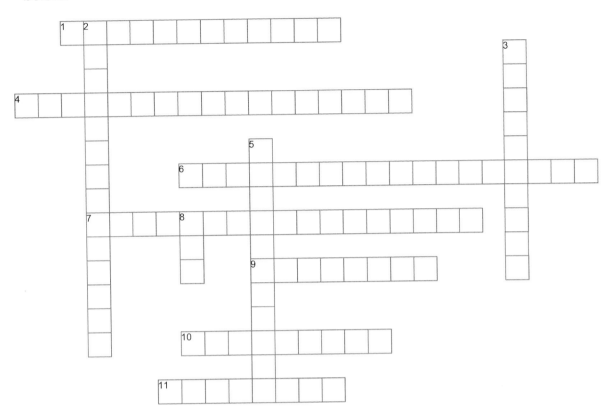

ACROSS

1. Amount of blood ejected with each ventricular contraction.
4. A test that measures and records the electrical activity in the heart.
6. An abnormal, very fast and disorganized heart rate with chaotic electrical activity in the atria of the heart.
7. A form of ultrasound that can detect blood flow. Used to diagnose cardiac disease.
9. Absence of a heartbeat, also known as "flat line". A dire condition in which the heart has no rhythm.
10. Cells within the heart that can initiate depolarization; external mechanical device that initiates cardiac depolarization.
11. A technique to remove or render inactive problematic cardiac tissue.

DOWN

2. One-way valve that allow blood flow from Right Atrium to Right Ventricle.
3. An abnormality or irregularity in the heart rhythm.
5. A pause caused by the SA node not firing; pause measures more than 2 R-R intervals.
8. Coronary artery that supplies oxygenated blood to the anterior surface of the left ventricle, the ventricular septum, and the papillary muscles of the mitral valve and the bundle of His.

A. Asystole
E. Atrial Fibrillation
I. Pacemaker

B. Stroke Volume
F. LAD
J. Arrhythmia

C. Tricuspid Valve
G. Ablation
K. Electrocardiogram

D. Sinus Arrest
H. Doppler Ultrasound

© 2017 Network4Learning, Inc.

15. *Using the Across and Down clues, write the correct words in the numbered grid below.*

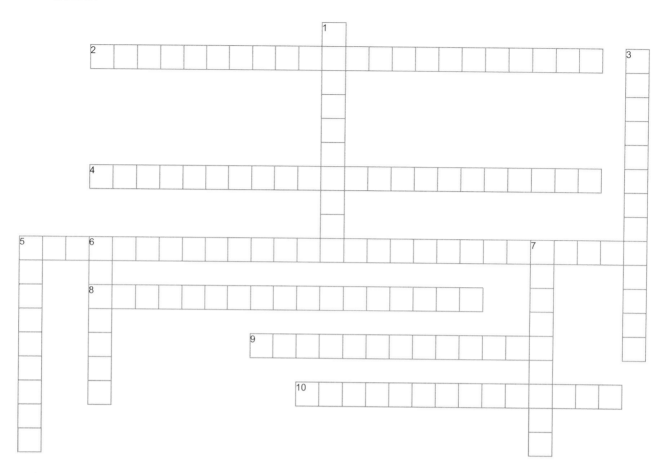

ACROSS

2. Impulse for ventricular contraction originated from ventricle with a rate of > 100pbm.

4. A fast heart rhythm that originates in the ventricles. Also known as V-tach.

5. Tachycardia with rate > 150bpm; no P waves can be identified.

8. A normal heart rate.

9. A medical device used to treat a victim with a life-threatening irregular heart rhythm.

10. Return of membrane potential to its resting state. K+ move into the cell and Na+ moves out.

DOWN

1. Measured from where the P-wave starts to where the QRS first leaves the isoelectric line. Represents atrial depolarization and the delay in the AV node.

3. Premature Ventricular contractions that originate from more than one focus.

5. A cluster of cells in the upper right atrium that generates electrical impulses and stimulates the heart to contract and pump blood.

6. A PVC that falls on or very near the T wave.

7. A set of precise rules programmed into a defibrillator to analyze heart rhythms and treat cardiac arrest.

A. Defibrillator
D. Sinus Node
G. Ventricular Tachycardia
J. Repolarization

B. Normal Sinus Rhythm
E. Algorithm
H. Supraventricular Tachycardia
K. R ON T PVC

C. Ventricular Tachycardia
F. Multifocal PVC
I. PR interval

© 2017 Network4Learning, Inc.

16. *Using the Across and Down clues, write the correct words in the numbered grid below.*

ACROSS

3. Innervates all parts of the heart and all the blood vessels.

6. Immunity protection provided by each state government and the Federal government to encourage lay responders to treat a victim of sudden cardiac arrest with an AED and CPR.

8. Coronary artery that delivers oxygenated blood to the left side of the heart. Divides into the left anterior descending artery and the circumflex artery.

9. Junction rhythm with a rate > 100bpm

10. Death as a result of sudden cardiac arrest.

11. Antiarrhythmic infusion for stable wide QRS Tachycardia. Used to treat life-threatening ventricular tachycardia or symptomatic PVC's.

DOWN

1. Part of the ECG complex that reflects atrial depolarization.

2. A medical device used to treat a victim with a life-threatening irregular heart rhythm.

4. A medical term to describe the normal beating of the heart.

5. A heart block where some P waves not conducted through AV node. Some P waves not followed by QRS complexes. P waves that do follow QRS, have consistent intervals.

7. cardiopulmonary resuscitation.

A. Junctional Tachycardia
D. P Wave
G. Defibrillator
J. Sudden Cardiac Death

B. Left Coronary Artery
E. Procainamide
H. Good Samaritan
K. CPR

C. Mobitz II
F. Sinus Rhythm
I. Sympathetic Nervous System

© 2017 Network4Learning, Inc.

17. *Using the Across and Down clues, write the correct words in the numbered grid below.*

ACROSS

2. cardiopulmonary resuscitation.

4. Constriction of the heart that prevent filling of the ventricles. It is usually caused by fluid or blood accumulating in the pericardial sac.

8. Sympathomimetic agent that causes peripheral vasoconstriction (alpha effects) and muscle vasodilation (beta effects).

9. PVC that occurs with every other beat.

10. Meets criteria for NSR except rhythm is irregular.

11. An unusually large heart. This condition can be a a result of conditions such as an abnormal heart rhythm, stress, or weakening of the heart muscle.

12. The sudden, unexpected loss of the heart function, resulting in the loss of effective blood flow.

DOWN

1. Used for heart block and ventricular arrhythmias. A sympathomimetic that results in pronounced stimulation of beta1 & beta2 receptors of heart and bronchi.

3. Final part of the conduction system that initiates vent. depolarization.

5. A set of precise rules programmed into a defibrillator to analyze heart rhythms and treat cardiac arrest.

6. A heart block where some P waves not conducted through AV node. Some P waves not followed by QRS complexes. P waves that do follow QRS, have consistent intervals.

7. Low pressure chamber that receives oxygenated blood from the pulmonary system via the pulmonary veins.

A. Left Atrium
D. Sudden Cardiac Arrest
G. Sinus Arrhythmia
J. Isuprel

B. Cardiac Tamponade
E. Purkinje Fibers
H. Mobitz II
K. CPR

C. Algorithm
F. Enlarged Heart
I. Ventricular Bigeminy
L. Dopamine

© 2017 Network4Learning, Inc.

18. *Using the Across and Down clues, write the correct words in the numbered grid below.*

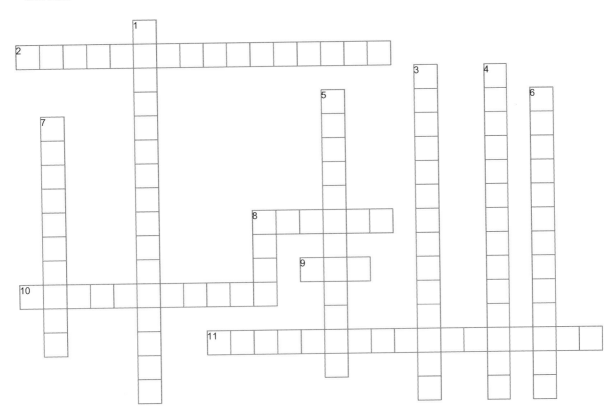

ACROSS

2. Constriction of the heart that prevent filling of the ventricles. It is usually caused by fluid or blood accumulating in the pericardial sac.

8. The upper chamber of each half of the heart.

9. Coronary artery that supplies oxygenated blood to the anterior surface of the left ventricle, the ventricular septum, and the papillary muscles of the mitral valve and the bundle of His.

10. Conducts impulses from AV node to bundle branches; makes up AV junction

11. polymorphic ventricular tachycardia characterized by QRS complexes that change directions.

DOWN

1. A forceful attempt at expiration when the airway is closed to stop supraventricular tachycardia.

3. Final part of the conduction system that initiates vent. depolarization.

4. The act of using equipment to send an electrical shock to the heart to stop an irregular heart rhythm. Defibrillation is the only cure to sudden cardiac arrest.

5. Antiarrhythmic infusion for stable wide QRS Tachycardia. Used to treat life-threatening ventricular tachycardia or symptomatic PVC's.

6. A medical device used to treat a victim with a life-threatening irregular heart rhythm.

7. Pause caused by delay in impulse being initiated in the SA node. pause is < 2 R-R intervals.

8. A series of advanced treatments for cardiac arrest and other life-threatening conditions.

A. ACLS
E. Cardiac Tamponade
I. LAD
B. Defibrillator
F. Valsalva Maneuver
J. Sinus Pause
C. Torsades de Pointes
G. Purkinje Fibers
K. Procainamide
D. Bundle of His
H. Atrium
L. Defibrillation

© 2017 Network4Learning, Inc.

19. *Using the Across and Down clues, write the correct words in the numbered grid below.*

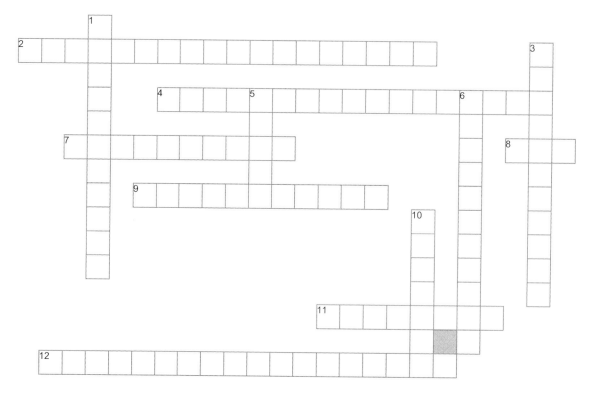

ACROSS

2. An abnormal, very fast and disorganized heart rate with chaotic electrical activity in the atria of the heart.

4. Rhythms initiated from impulses that originate from the Atrial Ventricular junction. Intrinsic rate 40-60bpm.

7. Measured from where the P-wave starts to where the QRS first leaves the isoelectric line. Represents atrial depolarization and the delay in the AV node.

8. cardiopulmonary resuscitation.

9. Conducts impulses from AV node to bundle branches; makes up AV junction

11. A heart block where some P waves not conducted through AV node. Some P waves not followed by QRS complexes. P waves that do follow QRS, have consistent intervals.

12. Coronary artery that delivers oxygenated blood to the left side of the heart. Divides into the left anterior descending artery and the circumflex artery.

DOWN

1. A medical term to describe the normal beating of the heart.

3. Alternate with epinephrine in patient with pulseless VFib

5. Ventricular repolarization; follows the QRS complex.

6. A rapid heart rate, usually over 100 beats per minute.

10. A rapid, but organized vibration of the heart muscle. Atrial flutter can result in 250-350 heart beats per minute.

A. Vasopressin
E. T wave
I. Mobitz II

B. Left Coronary Artery
F. Bundle of His
J. Atrial Fibrillation

C. CPR
G. PR interval
K. Tachycardia

D. Flutter
H. Sinus Rhythm
L. Junctional Rhythms

© 2017 Network4Learning, Inc.

20. *Using the Across and Down clues, write the correct words in the numbered grid below.*

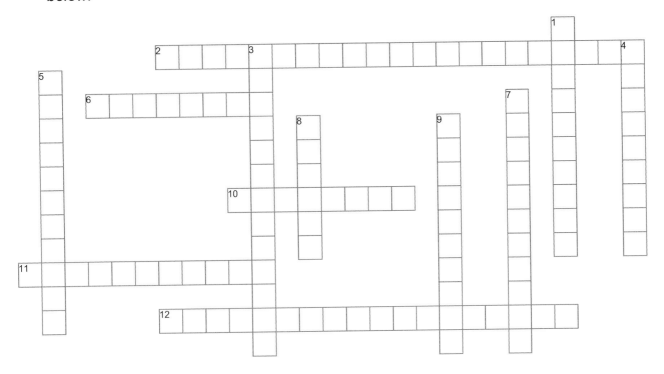

ACROSS

2. Junction rhythm with a rate > 100bpm
6. A thin, flexible tube that is inserted into the heart through a peripheral blood vessel to provide therapy and
10. A heart block where some P waves not conducted through AV node. Some P waves not followed by QRS complexes. P waves that do follow QRS, have consistent intervals.
11. A pause caused by the SA node not firing; pause measures more than 2 R-R intervals.
12. Coronary artery that delivers oxygenated blood to the left side of the heart. Divides into the left anterior descending artery and the circumflex artery.

DOWN

1. Smooth ridges on the walls of the heart.
3. A kind of drug that can break up or dissolve clots blocking the flow of blood to the heart muscle. Ideally, the drug should be administered within 90 minutes of being admitted for a heart attack.
4. Used to treat unstable tachy-arrhythmias if regular and monomorphic; Slows atrial conduction through AV node.
5. The amount of time it takes for ventricle depolarization. Measured from when the QRS first leaves the isoelectric line to where the ST segment begins.
7. Used in stable symptomatic tachycardia that is persistent and does not have a wide QRS.
8. The upper chamber of each half of the heart.
9. Measured from where the P-wave starts to where the QRS first leaves the isoelectric line. Represents atrial depolarization and the delay in the AV node.

A. Catheter
D. Beta blocker
G. Adenosine
J. PR interval

B. Atrium
E. Trabeculae
H. QRS Duration
K. Mobitz II

C. Left Coronary Artery
F. Junctional Tachycardia
I. Thrombolytics
L. Sinus Arrest

© 2017 Network4Learning, Inc.

1. *Using the Across and Down clues, write the correct words in the numbered grid below.*

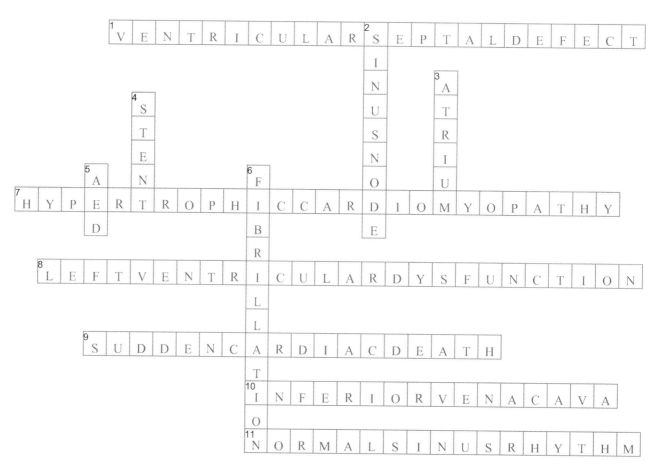

ACROSS

1. A congenital heart defect where an abnormal opening in the septum separates the ventricles.

7. A genetic disorder of the heart in which the heart muscle becomes abnormally thick, making it harder to pump blood.

8. A condition in which the left ventricle of the heart exhibits decreased functionality. This can lead to heart failure.

9. Death as a result of sudden cardiac arrest.

10. Large vein that carries deoxygenated blood from the lower venous circulation (below the neck) and empties into the Right Atrium.

11. A normal heart rate.

DOWN

2. A cluster of cells in the upper right atrium that generates electrical impulses and stimulates the heart to contract and pump blood.

3. The upper chamber of each half of the heart.

4. A tube designed to be implanted in a vessel to help keep it open.

5. A life-saving device that treats sudden cardiac arrest.

6. A rapid twitching of the heart muscles caused by an abnormal and sometimes chaotic discharge of electrical impulses. Atrial fibrillation results in a rapid and irregular heartbeat.

A. Sinus Node
D. Atrium
G. Normal Sinus Rhythm
J. Stent

B. Fibrillation
E. AED
H. Ventricular Septal Defect
K. Hypertrophic Cardiomyopathy

C. Left Ventricular Dysfunction
F. Sudden Cardiac Death
I. Inferior Vena Cava

© 2017 Network4Learning, Inc.

2. *Using the Across and Down clues, write the correct words in the numbered grid below.*

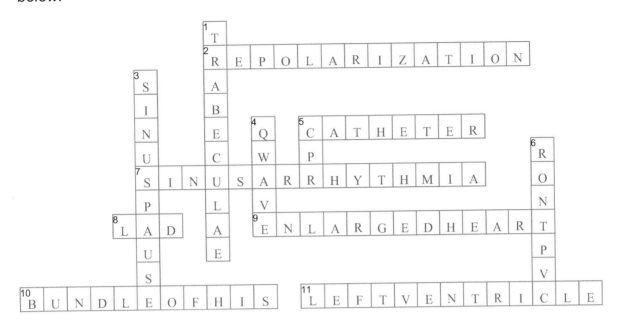

ACROSS

2. Return of membrane potential to its resting state. K+ move into the cell and Na+ moves out.

5. A thin, flexible tube that is inserted into the heart through a peripheral blood vessel to provide therapy and

7. Meets criteria for NSR except rhythm is irregular.

8. Coronary artery that supplies oxygenated blood to the anterior surface of the left ventricle, the ventricular septum, and the papillary muscles of the mitral valve and the bundle of His.

9. An unusually large heart. This condition can be a a result of conditions such as an abnormal heart rhythm, stress, or weakening of the heart muscle.

10. Conducts impulses from AV node to bundle branches; makes up AV junction

11. High pressure chamber of the heart responsible for pumping oxygenated blood to the systemic circulation.

DOWN

1. Smooth ridges on the walls of the heart.

3. Pause caused by delay in impulse being initiated in the SA node. pause is < 2 R-R intervals.

4. The first negative deflection following the P wave.

5. cardiopulmonary resuscitation.

6. A PVC that falls on or very near the T wave.

A. Sinus Arrhythmia
E. Bundle of His
I. Sinus Pause
B. R ON T PVC
F. Catheter
J. Left Ventricle
C. Trabeculae
G. Enlarged Heart
K. LAD
D. CPR
H. Repolarization
L. Q wave

© 2017 Network4Learning, Inc.

3. *Using the Across and Down clues, write the correct words in the numbered grid below.*

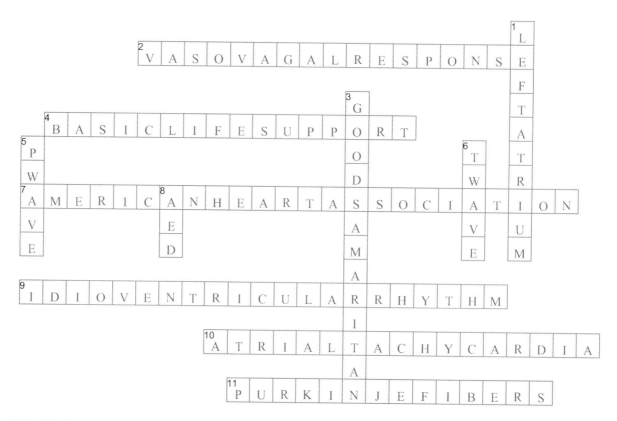

ACROSS

2. Caused by stimulation of para-sympathetic Nervous System and results in slowing of the Heart Rate. Can be initiated intentionally with carotid massage or valsalva maneuver.

4. Fundamental treatment provided to a victim to include CPR and AED use.

7. A non-profit organization that establishes the standards in cardiac care.

9. Originates in the ventricle. Rate is 20-40bpm.

10. A rapid heart rhythm resulting in 160-190 beats per minute and is a type of supraventricular tachycardia.

11. Final part of the conduction system that initiates vent. depolarization.

DOWN

1. The upper left chamber of the heart that receives oxygenated blood from the lungs and pumps it to the left ventricle.

3. Immunity protection provided by each state government and the Federal government to encourage lay responders to treat a victim of sudden cardiac arrest with an AED and CPR.

5. Part of the ECG complex that reflects atrial depolarization.

6. Ventricular repolarization; follows the QRS complex.

8. A life-saving device that treats sudden cardiac arrest.

A. P Wave	B. American Heart Association	C. AED
D. Vasovagal Response	E. Idioventricular Rhythm	F. Good Samaritan
G. Basic Life Support	H. Purkinje Fibers	I. Atrial Tachycardia
J. Left Atrium	K. T wave	

© 2017 Network4Learning, Inc.

4. *Using the Across and Down clues, write the correct words in the numbered grid below.*

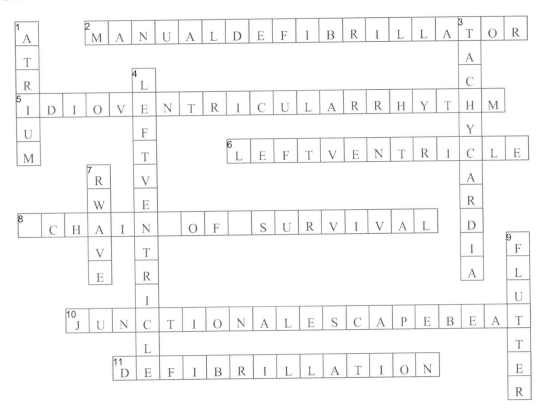

ACROSS

2. An advanced life support medical device that monitors the heart rhythm and allow the user to manually set the energy delivery and deliver a shock.

5. Originates in the ventricle. Rate is 20-40bpm.

6. High pressure chamber of the heart responsible for pumping oxygenated blood to the systemic circulation.

8. A four-step process for treating victims of sudden cardiac arrest.

10. Complex or rhythm that takes over if SA node fails. Beats or rhythm occur after a pause and later than expected.

11. The act of using equipment to send an electrical shock to the heart to stop an irregular heart rhythm. Defibrillation is the only cure to sudden cardiac arrest.

DOWN

1. The upper chamber of each half of the heart.

3. A rapid heart rate, usually over 100 beats per minute.

4. The lower left chamber of the heart that receives oxygenated blood from the left atrium and pumps the blood through the aorta to the body.

7. The 1st positive deflection following the P wave.

9. A rapid, but organized vibration of the heart muscle. Atrial flutter can result in 250-350 heart beats per minute.

A. Chain of Survival
D. Idioventricular Rhythm
G. Left Ventricle
J. R wave

B. Junctional Escape Beat
E. Left Ventricle
H. Flutter
K. Manual Defibrillator

C. Atrium
F. Defibrillation
I. Tachycardia

© 2017 Network4Learning, Inc.

5. *Using the Across and Down clues, write the correct words in the numbered grid below.*

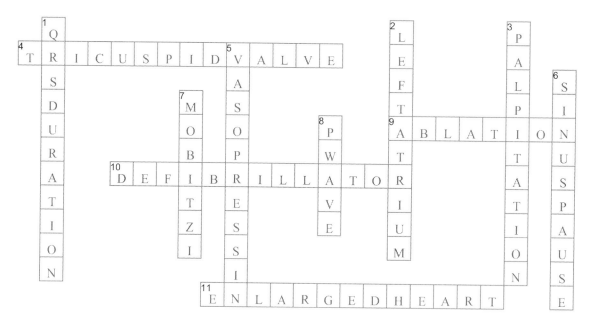

ACROSS

4. One-way valve that allow blood flow from Right Atrium to Right Ventricle.

9. A technique to remove or render inactive problematic cardiac tissue.

10. A medical device used to treat a victim with a life-threatening irregular heart rhythm.

11. An unusually large heart. This condition can be a a result of conditions such as an abnormal heart rhythm, stress, or weakening of the heart muscle.

DOWN

1. The amount of time it takes for ventricle depolarization. Measured from when the QRS first leaves the isoelectric line to where the ST segment begins.

2. Low pressure chamber that receives oxygenated blood from the pulmonary system via the pulmonary veins.

3. Rapid, fluttering heart beats. Heart palpitations can be triggered by exercise, medications, or stress.

5. Alternate with epinephrine in patient with pulseless VFib

6. Pause caused by delay in impulse being initiated in the SA node. pause is < 2 R-R intervals.

7. A heart block where the PR interval becomes progressively longer until the P wave is not conducted through the ventricle and a QRS complex is dropped.

8. Part of the ECG complex that reflects atrial depolarization.

A. Vasopressin
E. Palpitation
I. Enlarged Heart

B. Tricuspid Valve
F. Mobitz I
J. Ablation

C. Sinus Pause
G. QRS Duration
K. Left Atrium

D. Defibrillator
H. P Wave

© 2017 Network4Learning, Inc.

6. *Using the Across and Down clues, write the correct words in the numbered grid below.*

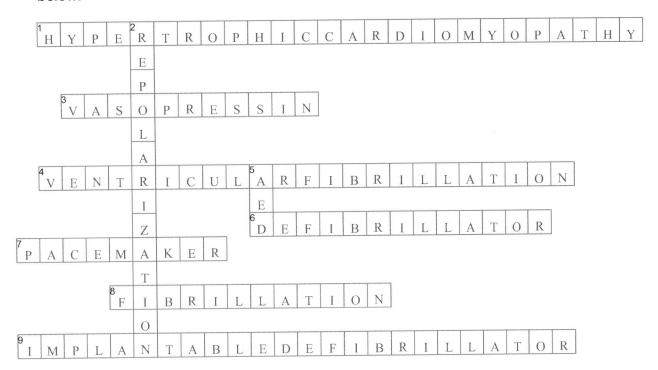

ACROSS

1. A genetic disorder of the heart in which the heart muscle becomes abnormally thick, making it harder to pump blood.

3. Alternate with epinephrine in patient with pulseless VFib

4. Weak disorganized quivering of the ventricle with no identifying QRS complex.

6. A medical device used to treat a victim with a life-threatening irregular heart rhythm.

7. An implantable medical device that sends electrical signals to the heart to set the heart rhythm.

8. A rapid twitching of the heart muscles caused by an abnormal and sometimes chaotic discharge of electrical impulses. Atrial fibrillation results in a rapid and irregular heartbeat.

9. A medical device that is implanted in the body to diagnose and treat abnormal electrical arrhythmias. If an abnormal arrhythmia is detected, the ICD will apply a shock to restore the heart to a normal rhythm.

DOWN

2. Return of membrane potential to its resting state. K+ move into the cell and Na+ moves out.

5. A life-saving device that treats sudden cardiac arrest.

A. Fibrillation
D. Ventricular Fibrillation
G. Implantable Defibrillator

B. Defibrillator
E. Vasopressin
H. Pacemaker

C. Repolarization
F. Hypertrophic Cardiomyopathy
I. AED

© 2017 Network4Learning, Inc.

7. *Using the Across and Down clues, write the correct words in the numbered grid below.*

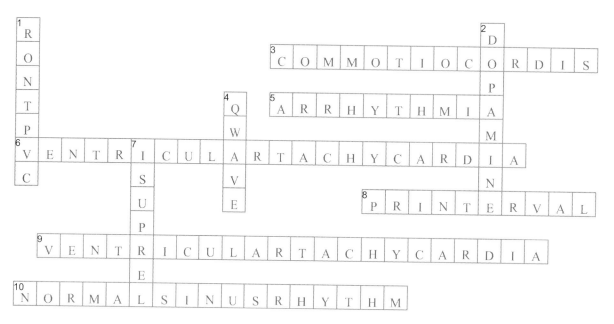

ACROSS

3. A disruption of the heart rhythm caused by a sudden blunt blow to the chest.

5. An abnormality or irregularity in the heart rhythm.

6. Impulse for ventricular contraction originated from ventricle with a rate of > 100pbm.

8. Measured from where the P-wave starts to where the QRS first leaves the isoelectric line. Represents atrial depolarization and the delay in the AV node.

9. A fast heart rhythm that originates in the ventricles. Also known as V-tach.

10. A normal heart rate.

DOWN

1. A PVC that falls on or very near the T wave.

2. Sympathomimetic agent that causes peripheral vasoconstriction (alpha effects) and muscle vasodilation (beta effects).

4. The first negative deflection following the P wave.

7. Used for heart block and ventricular arrhythmias. A sympathomimetic that results in pronounced stimulation of beta1 & beta2 receptors of heart and bronchi.

A. PR interval
D. Ventricular Tachycardia
G. Arrhythmia
J. Q wave

B. Commotio Cordis
E. Ventricular Tachycardia
H. R ON T PVC

C. Normal Sinus Rhythm
F. Isuprel
I. Dopamine

© 2017 Network4Learning, Inc.

8. *Using the Across and Down clues, write the correct words in the numbered grid below.*

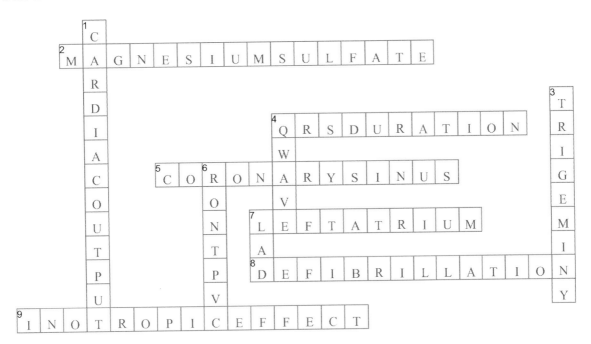

ACROSS

2. Treats Torsades de Pointes, Ventricular Fibrillation. Electrolyte that causes all muscles to contract. Results in depression early after depolarization.

4. The amount of time it takes for ventricle depolarization. Measured from when the QRS first leaves the isoelectric line to where the ST segment begins.

5. Venous drainage system of the heart. Returns de-oxygenated blood from the heart to the Right Atrium.

7. The upper left chamber of the heart that receives oxygenated blood from the lungs and pumps it to the left ventricle.

8. The act of using equipment to send an electrical shock to the heart to stop an irregular heart rhythm. Defibrillation is the only cure to sudden cardiac arrest.

9. Increases force of muscle contraction.

DOWN

1. The amount of blood ejected by the heart in one minute in liters

3. Premature ventricular contractions occurring every third beat.

4. The first negative deflection following the P wave.

6. A PVC that falls on or very near the T wave.

7. Coronary artery that supplies oxygenated blood to the anterior surface of the left ventricle, the ventricular septum, and the papillary muscles of the mitral valve and the bundle of His.

A. Left Atrium
E. QRS Duration
I. Defibrillation
B. Coronary Sinus
F. Inotropic Effect
J. Cardiac Output
C. LAD
G. Trigeminy
K. Magnesium sulfate
D. Q wave
H. R ON T PVC

© 2017 Network4Learning, Inc.

9. *Using the Across and Down clues, write the correct words in the numbered grid below.*

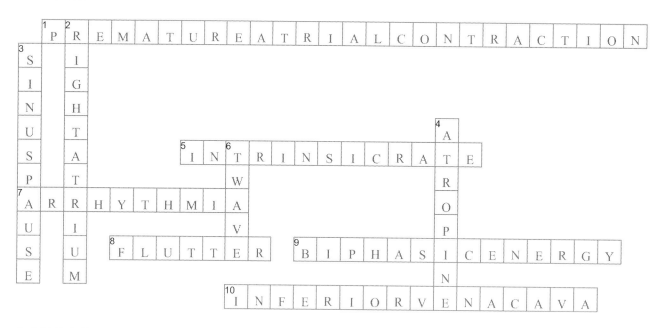

ACROSS

1. An ECG complex that appears earlier than expected; originates from ectopic focus in atrium.

5. The normal rate for a given pacemaker cells.

7. An abnormality or irregularity in the heart rhythm.

8. A rapid, but organized vibration of the heart muscle. Atrial flutter can result in 250-350 heart beats per minute.

9. Current from a defibrillator is delivered two ways. Biphasic therapy was introduced in the 1990s and lowers the electrical threshold for successful defibrillation.

10. Large vein that carries deoxygenated blood from the lower venous circulation (below the neck) and empties into the Right Atrium.

DOWN

2. Low pressure cardiac chamber that receives deoxygenated blood from the systemic venous circulation via the inferior vena cava and the superior vena cava.

3. Pause caused by delay in impulse being initiated in the SA node. pause is < 2 R-R intervals.

4. Para-sympatholytic that blocks acetylcholine effects on post cholinergic receptors in smooth muscle and SA -AV nodes.

6. Ventricular repolarization; follows the QRS complex.

A. Arrhythmia
D. T wave
G. Sinus Pause
J. Biphasic Energy

B. Atropine
E. Right Atrium
H. Inferior Vena Cava

C. Flutter
F. Premature Atrial Contraction
I. Intrinsic Rate

© 2017 Network4Learning, Inc.

10. *Using the Across and Down clues, write the correct words in the numbered grid below.*

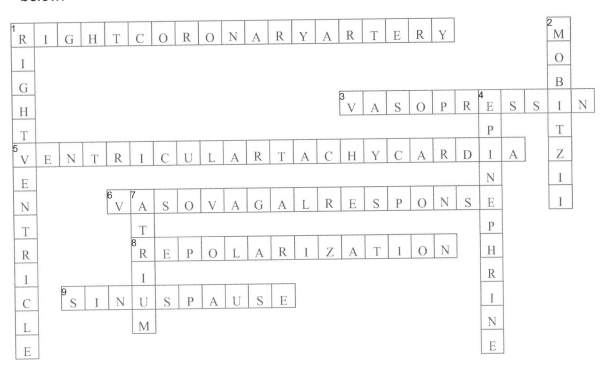

ACROSS

1. Coronary artery that delivers blood to the Right Ventricle, AV junction, and the SA node in 55% of the population.

3. Alternate with epinephrine in patient with pulseless VFib

5. A fast heart rhythm that originates in the ventricles. Also known as V-tach.

6. Caused by stimulation of para-sympathetic Nervous System and results in slowing of the Heart Rate. Can be initiated intentionally with carotid massage or valsalva maneuver.

8. Return of membrane potential to its resting state. K+ move into the cell and Na+ moves out.

9. Pause caused by delay in impulse being initiated in the SA node. pause is < 2 R-R intervals.

DOWN

1. Low pressure cardiac chamber that receives blood from the Right Atrium and pumps it into the pulmonary artery.

2. A heart block where some P waves not conducted through AV node. Some P waves not followed by QRS complexes. P waves that do follow QRS, have consistent intervals.

4. Sympathomimetic that stimulates alpha, beta 1&2 receptors resulting in cardiac stimulation.

7. The upper chamber of each half of the heart.

A. Atrium
D. Sinus Pause
G. Repolarization
J. Right Coronary Artery

B. Mobitz II
E. Epinephrine
H. Vasopressin

C. Ventricular Tachycardia
F. Right Ventricle
I. Vasovagal Response

© 2017 Network4Learning, Inc.

11. *Using the Across and Down clues, write the correct words in the numbered grid below.*

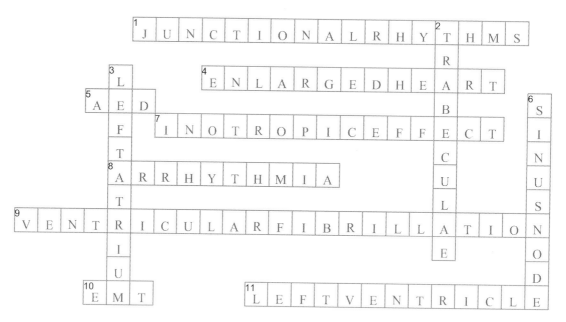

ACROSS

1. Rhythms initiated from impulses that originate from the Atrial Ventricular junction. Intrinsic rate 40-60bpm.

4. An unusually large heart. This condition can be a a result of conditions such as an abnormal heart rhythm, stress, or weakening of the heart muscle.

5. A life-saving device that treats sudden cardiac arrest.

7. Increases force of muscle contraction.

8. An abnormality or irregularity in the heart rhythm.

9. The most common form of sudden cardiac arrest. A sudden, lethal arrhythmia in which chaotic electrical activity results in the ventricles fluttering rapidly and losing the ability to pump blood.

10. A trained and certified professional who can use advanced life support techniques to treat sudden cardiac arrest.

11. High pressure chamber of the heart responsible for pumping oxygenated blood to the systemic circulation.

DOWN

2. Smooth ridges on the walls of the heart.

3. Low pressure chamber that receives oxygenated blood from the pulmonary system via the pulmonary veins.

6. A cluster of cells in the upper right atrium that generates electrical impulses and stimulates the heart to contract and pump blood.

A. AED
D. Junctional Rhythms
G. EMT
J. Arrhythmia

B. Left Atrium
E. Inotropic Effect
H. Trabeculae
K. Enlarged Heart

C. Sinus Node
F. Ventricular Fibrillation
I. Left Ventricle

© 2017 Network4Learning, Inc.

12. *Using the Across and Down clues, write the correct words in the numbered grid below.*

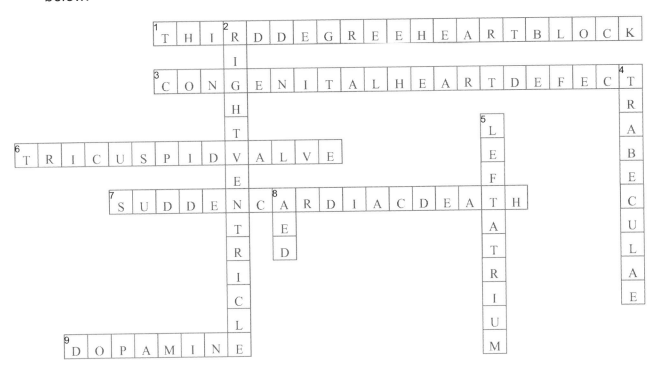

ACROSS

1. Independent activity of atria and ventricles
3. A birth defect of the heart
6. One-way valve that allow blood flow from Right Atrium to Right Ventricle.
7. Death as a result of sudden cardiac arrest.
9. Sympathomimetic agent that causes peripheral vasoconstriction (alpha effects) and muscle vasodilation (beta effects).

DOWN

2. The lower right chamber of the heart that receives deoxygenated blood from the right atrium and pumps it to the lungs through the pulmonary artery.
4. Smooth ridges on the walls of the heart.
5. Low pressure chamber that receives oxygenated blood from the pulmonary system via the pulmonary veins.
8. A life-saving device that treats sudden cardiac arrest.

A. Right Ventricle
D. Trabeculae
G. Tricuspid Valve
B. Congenital Heart Defect
E. Left Atrium
H. Sudden Cardiac Death
C. Third degree Heart Block
F. Dopamine
I. AED

© 2017 Network4Learning, Inc.

13. *Using the Across and Down clues, write the correct words in the numbered grid below.*

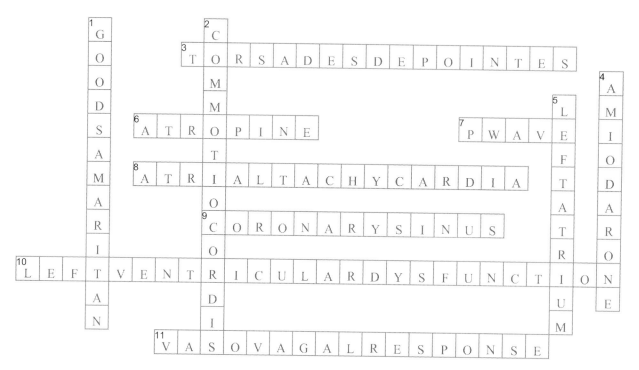

ACROSS

3. polymorphic ventricular tachycardia characterized by QRS complexes that change directions.

6. Para-sympatholytic that blocks acetylcholine effects on post cholinergic receptors in smooth muscle and SA-AV nodes.

7. Part of the ECG complex that reflects atrial depolarization.

8. A rapid heart rhythm resulting in 160-190 beats per minute and is a type of supraventricular tachycardia.

9. Venous drainage system of the heart. Returns de-oxygenated blood from the heart to the Right Atrium.

10. A condition in which the left ventricle of the heart exhibits decreased functionality. This can lead to heart failure.

11. Caused by stimulation of para-sympathetic Nervous System and results in slowing of the Heart Rate. Can be initiated intentionally with carotid massage or valsalva maneuver.

DOWN

1. Immunity protection provided by each state government and the Federal government to encourage lay responders to treat a victim of sudden cardiac arrest with an AED and CPR.

2. A disruption of the heart rhythm caused by a sudden blunt blow to the chest.

4. Anti-arrhythmic used to treat atrial-ventricular tachyarrhythmias.

5. Low pressure chamber that receives oxygenated blood from the pulmonary system via the pulmonary veins.

A. Good Samaritan
D. Commotio Cordis
G. Coronary Sinus
J. P Wave

B. Left Atrium
E. Torsades de Pointes
H. Atrial Tachycardia
K. Atropine

C. Left Ventricular Dysfunction
F. Amiodarone
I. Vasovagal Response

© 2017 Network4Learning, Inc.

14. *Using the Across and Down clues, write the correct words in the numbered grid below.*

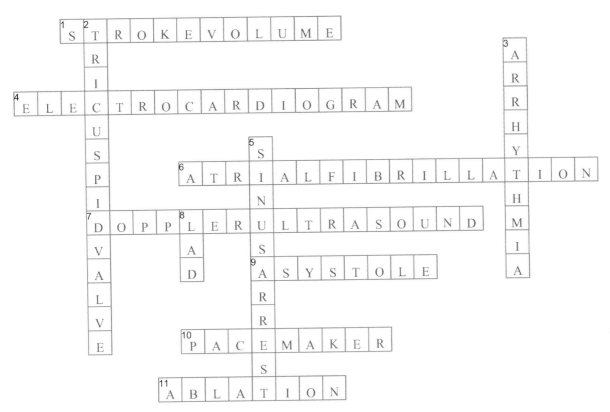

ACROSS

1. Amount of blood ejected with each ventricular contraction.

4. A test that measures and records the electrical activity in the heart.

6. An abnormal, very fast and disorganized heart rate with chaotic electrical activity in the atria of the heart.

7. A form of ultrasound that can detect blood flow. Used to diagnose cardiac disease.

9. Absence of a heartbeat, also known as "flat line". A dire condition in which the heart has no rhythm.

10. Cells within the heart that can initiate depolarization; external mechanical device that initiates cardiac depolarization.

11. A technique to remove or render inactive problematic cardiac tissue.

DOWN

2. One-way valve that allow blood flow from Right Atrium to Right Ventricle.

3. An abnormality or irregularity in the heart rhythm.

5. A pause caused by the SA node not firing; pause measures more than 2 R-R intervals.

8. Coronary artery that supplies oxygenated blood to the anterior surface of the left ventricle, the ventricular septum, and the papillary muscles of the mitral valve and the bundle of His.

A. Asystole
E. Atrial Fibrillation
I. Pacemaker

B. Stroke Volume
F. LAD
J. Arrhythmia

C. Tricuspid Valve
G. Ablation
K. Electrocardiogram

D. Sinus Arrest
H. Doppler Ultrasound

© 2017 Network4Learning, Inc.

15. *Using the Across and Down clues, write the correct words in the numbered grid below.*

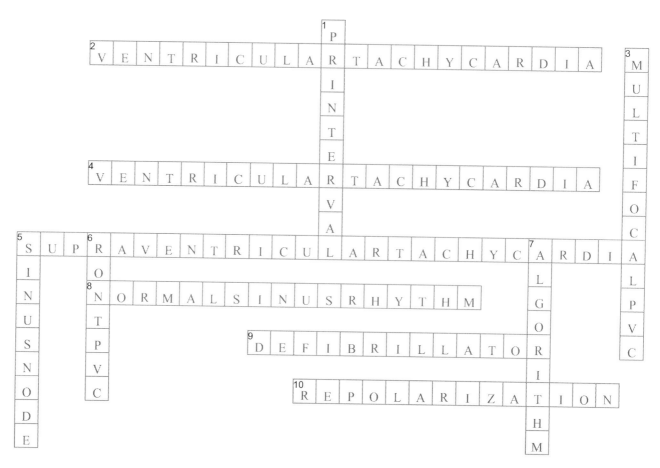

ACROSS

2. Impulse for ventricular contraction originated from ventricle with a rate of > 100pbm.

4. A fast heart rhythm that originates in the ventricles. Also known as V-tach.

5. Tachycardia with rate > 150bpm; no P waves can be identified.

8. A normal heart rate.

9. A medical device used to treat a victim with a life-threatening irregular heart rhythm.

10. Return of membrane potential to its resting state. K+ move into the cell and Na+ moves out.

DOWN

1. Measured from where the P-wave starts to where the QRS first leaves the isoelectric line. Represents atrial depolarization and the delay in the AV node.

3. Premature Ventricular contractions that originate from more than one focus.

5. A cluster of cells in the upper right atrium that generates electrical impulses and stimulates the heart to contract and pump blood.

6. A PVC that falls on or very near the T wave.

7. A set of precise rules programmed into a defibrillator to analyze heart rhythms and treat cardiac arrest.

A. Defibrillator
D. Sinus Node
G. Ventricular Tachycardia
J. Repolarization

B. Normal Sinus Rhythm
E. Algorithm
H. Supraventricular Tachycardia
K. R ON T PVC

C. Ventricular Tachycardia
F. Multifocal PVC
I. PR interval

© 2017 Network4Learning, Inc.

16. *Using the Across and Down clues, write the correct words in the numbered grid below.*

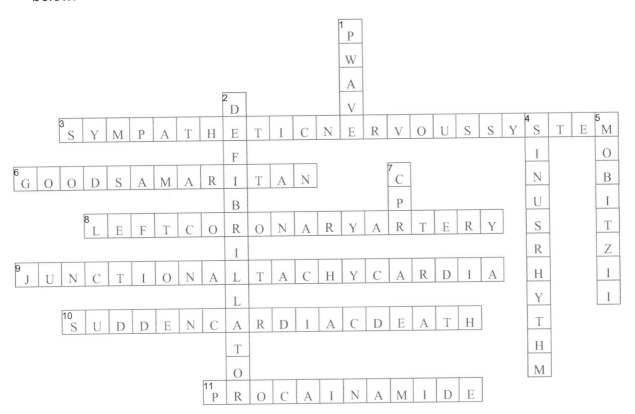

ACROSS

3. Innervates all parts of the heart and all the blood vessels.

6. Immunity protection provided by each state government and the Federal government to encourage lay responders to treat a victim of sudden cardiac arrest with an AED and CPR.

8. Coronary artery that delivers oxygenated blood to the left side of the heart. Divides into the left anterior descending artery and the circumflex artery.

9. Junction rhythm with a rate > 100bpm

10. Death as a result of sudden cardiac arrest.

11. Antiarrhythmic infusion for stable wide QRS Tachycardia. Used to treat life-threatening ventricular tachycardia or symptomatic PVC's.

DOWN

1. Part of the ECG complex that reflects atrial depolarization.

2. A medical device used to treat a victim with a life-threatening irregular heart rhythm.

4. A medical term to describe the normal beating of the heart.

5. A heart block where some P waves not conducted through AV node. Some P waves not followed by QRS complexes. P waves that do follow QRS, have consistent intervals.

7. cardiopulmonary resuscitation.

A. Junctional Tachycardia
D. P Wave
G. Defibrillator
J. Sudden Cardiac Death

B. Left Coronary Artery
E. Procainamide
H. Good Samaritan
K. CPR

C. Mobitz II
F. Sinus Rhythm
I. Sympathetic Nervous System

© 2017 Network4Learning, Inc.

17. *Using the Across and Down clues, write the correct words in the numbered grid below.*

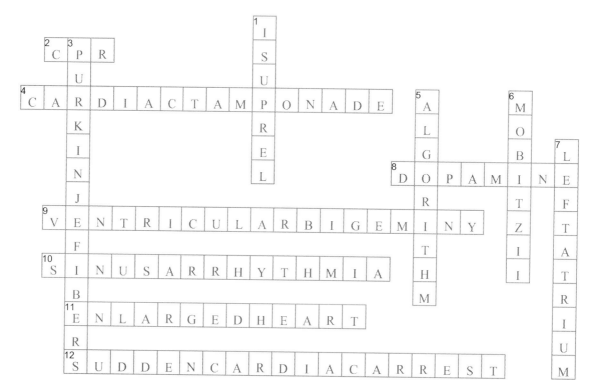

ACROSS

2. cardiopulmonary resuscitation.
4. Constriction of the heart that prevent filling of the ventricles. It is usually caused by fluid or blood accumulating in the pericardial sac.
8. Sympathomimetic agent that causes peripheral vasoconstriction (alpha effects) and muscle vasodilation (beta effects).
9. PVC that occurs with every other beat.
10. Meets criteria for NSR except rhythm is irregular.
11. An unusually large heart. This condition can be a a result of conditions such as an abnormal heart rhythm, stress, or weakening of the heart muscle.
12. The sudden, unexpected loss of the heart function, resulting in the loss of effective blood flow.

DOWN

1. Used for heart block and ventricular arrhythmias. A sympathomimetic that results in pronounced stimulation of beta1 & beta2 receptors of heart and bronchi.
3. Final part of the conduction system that initiates vent. depolarization.
5. A set of precise rules programmed into a defibrillator to analyze heart rhythms and treat cardiac arrest.
6. A heart block where some P waves not conducted through AV node. Some P waves not followed by QRS complexes. P waves that do follow QRS, have consistent intervals.
7. Low pressure chamber that receives oxygenated blood from the pulmonary system via the pulmonary veins.

A. Left Atrium
D. Sudden Cardiac Arrest
G. Sinus Arrhythmia
J. Isuprel

B. Cardiac Tamponade
E. Purkinje Fibers
H. Mobitz II
K. CPR

C. Algorithm
F. Enlarged Heart
I. Ventricular Bigeminy
L. Dopamine

© 2017 Network4Learning, Inc.

18. *Using the Across and Down clues, write the correct words in the numbered grid below.*

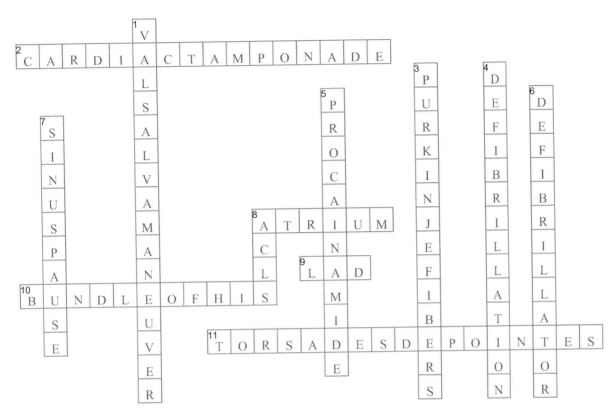

ACROSS

2. Constriction of the heart that prevent filling of the ventricles. It is usually caused by fluid or blood accumulating in the pericardial sac.

8. The upper chamber of each half of the heart.

9. Coronary artery that supplies oxygenated blood to the anterior surface of the left ventricle, the ventricular septum, and the papillary muscles of the mitral valve and the bundle of His.

10. Conducts impulses from AV node to bundle branches; makes up AV junction

11. polymorphic ventricular tachycardia characterized by QRS complexes that change directions.

DOWN

1. A forceful attempt at expiration when the airway is closed to stop supraventricular tachycardia.

3. Final part of the conduction system that initiates vent. depolarization.

4. The act of using equipment to send an electrical shock to the heart to stop an irregular heart rhythm. Defibrillation is the only cure to sudden cardiac arrest.

5. Antiarrhythmic infusion for stable wide QRS Tachycardia. Used to treat life-threatening ventricular tachycardia or symptomatic PVC's.

6. A medical device used to treat a victim with a life-threatening irregular heart rhythm.

7. Pause caused by delay in impulse being initiated in the SA node. pause is < 2 R-R intervals.

8. A series of advanced treatments for cardiac arrest and other life-threatening conditions.

A. ACLS
E. Cardiac Tamponade
I. LAD
B. Defibrillator
F. Valsalva Maneuver
J. Sinus Pause
C. Torsades de Pointes
G. Purkinje Fibers
K. Procainamide
D. Bundle of His
H. Atrium
L. Defibrillation

© 2017 Network4Learning, Inc.

19. *Using the Across and Down clues, write the correct words in the numbered grid below.*

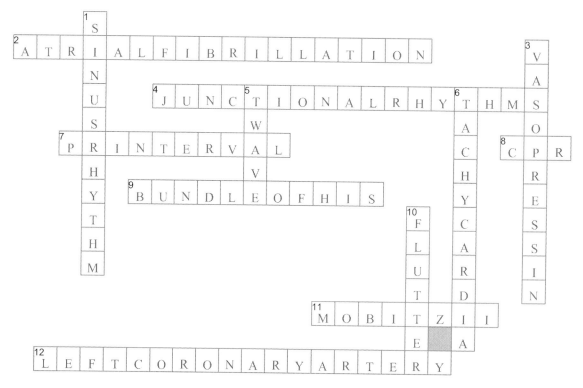

ACROSS

2. An abnormal, very fast and disorganized heart rate with chaotic electrical activity in the atria of the heart.

4. Rhythms initiated from impulses that originate from the Atrial Ventricular junction. Intrinsic rate 40-60bpm.

7. Measured from where the P-wave starts to where the QRS first leaves the isoelectric line. Represents atrial depolarization and the delay in the AV node.

8. cardiopulmonary resuscitation.

9. Conducts impulses from AV node to bundle branches; makes up AV junction

11. A heart block where some P waves not conducted through AV node. Some P waves not followed by QRS complexes. P waves that do follow QRS, have consistent intervals.

12. Coronary artery that delivers oxygenated blood to the left side of the heart. Divides into the left anterior descending artery and the circumflex artery.

DOWN

1. A medical term to describe the normal beating of the heart.

3. Alternate with epinephrine in patient with pulseless VFib

5. Ventricular repolarization; follows the QRS complex.

6. A rapid heart rate, usually over 100 beats per minute.

10. A rapid, but organized vibration of the heart muscle. Atrial flutter can result in 250-350 heart beats per minute.

A. Vasopressin
E. T wave
I. Mobitz II

B. Left Coronary Artery
F. Bundle of His
J. Atrial Fibrillation

C. CPR
G. PR interval
K. Tachycardia

D. Flutter
H. Sinus Rhythm
L. Junctional Rhythms

© 2017 Network4Learning, Inc.

20. *Using the Across and Down clues, write the correct words in the numbered grid below.*

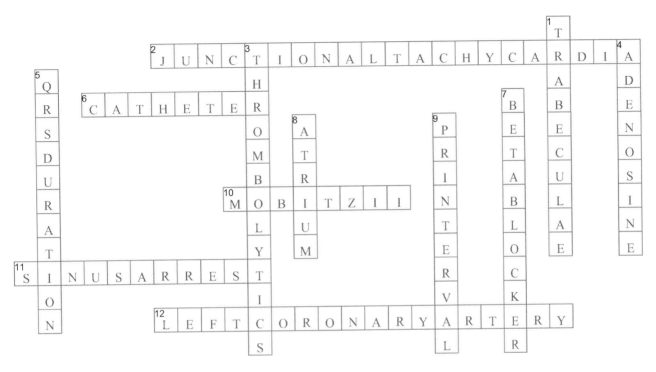

ACROSS

2. Junction rhythm with a rate > 100bpm

6. A thin, flexible tube that is inserted into the heart through a peripheral blood vessel to provide therapy and

10. A heart block where some P waves not conducted through AV node. Some P waves not followed by QRS complexes. P waves that do follow QRS, have consistent intervals.

11. A pause caused by the SA node not firing; pause measures more than 2 R-R intervals.

12. Coronary artery that delivers oxygenated blood to the left side of the heart. Divides into the left anterior descending artery and the circumflex artery.

DOWN

1. Smooth ridges on the walls of the heart.

3. A kind of drug that can break up or dissolve clots blocking the flow of blood to the heart muscle. Ideally, the drug should be administered within 90 minutes of being admitted for a heart attack.

4. Used to treat unstable tachy-arrhythmias if regular and monomorphic; Slows atrial conduction through AV node.

5. The amount of time it takes for ventricle depolarization. Measured from when the QRS first leaves the isoelectric line to where the ST segment begins.

7. Used in stable symptomatic tachycardia that is persistent and does not have a wide QRS.

8. The upper chamber of each half of the heart.

9. Measured from where the P-wave starts to where the QRS first leaves the isoelectric line. Represents atrial depolarization and the delay in the AV node.

A. Catheter
D. Beta blocker
G. Adenosine
J. PR interval

B. Atrium
E. Trabeculae
H. QRS Duration
K. Mobitz II

C. Left Coronary Artery
F. Junctional Tachycardia
I. Thrombolytics
L. Sinus Arrest

© 2017 Network4Learning, Inc.

Multiple Choice

From the words provided for each clue, provide the letter of the word which best matches the clue.

1. ___ Rapid, organized atrial contractions that usually result in a heart rate of 250-350 beats per minute. AF is a form of supraventricular tachycardia.
A.left coronary artery   B.thrombolytics   C.junctional rhythms   D.atrial flutter

2. ___ A form of ultrasound that can detect blood flow. Used to diagnose cardiac disease.
A.joules   B.inferior vena cava   C.algorithm   D.doppler ultrasound

3. ___ Ventricular repolarization; follows the QRS complex.
A.cardioversion   B.t wave   C.catheter   D.vasopressin

4. ___ cardiopulmonary resuscitation.
A.enlarged heart   B.implantable defibrillator   C.cpr   D.junctional rhythms

5. ___ Smooth ridges on the walls of the heart.
A.trabeculae   B.heart murmur   C.aed   D.third degree heart block

6. ___ A rapid rhythm of the heart, with a pulse of 150-250 beats per minute. The condition can last a few minutes or even days. Treatment may come in the form of cardioversion.
A.supraventricular tachycardia   B.implantable defibrillator   C.third degree heart block   D.solatol

7. ___ Vessel that delivers blood from the Left Ventricle to Pulmonary veins.
A.pacemaker   B.pulmonary artery   C.palpitation   D.cardioversion

8. ___ A cluster of cells in the upper right atrium that generates electrical impulses and stimulates the heart to contract and pump blood.
A.sinus node   B.emt   C.chronotropic effect   D.trabeculae

9. ___ A heart block where the PR interval becomes progressively longer until the P wave is not conducted through the ventricle and a QRS complex is dropped.
A.acls   B.mobitz i   C.flutter   D.electrophysiology

10. ___ A medical procedure by which a trained professional converts an abnormally fast heart rate to a normal rate using defibrillation.
A.inferior vena cava   B.american heart association   C.cardioversion   D.pericardial effusion

11. ___ An abnormality or irregularity in the heart rhythm.
A.chronotropic effect   B.solatol   C.arrhythmia   D.congenital heart defect

12. ___ Low pressure cardiac chamber that receives deoxygenated blood from the systemic venous circulation via the inferior vena cava and the superior vena cava.
A.right coronary artery   B.right atrium   C.sinus pause   D.myocardium

13. ___ Normal Sinus Rhythm with PR interval > 0.20.
A.r on t pvc   B.first degree block   C. chain of survival   D.sudden cardiac death

14. ___ Muscle layer of the heart.
A.myocardium   B.supraventricular tachycardia   C.sinus arrhythmia   D.arrhythmia

15. ___ Antiarrythmic infusion for stable wide QRS Tachycardia. Depresses heart rate, slows AV conduction, decreases cardiac output, and lowers systolic and diastolic blood pressure.
A.solatol   B.premature junctional contraction   C.cpr   D.supraventricular tachycardia

16. ___ An ECG complex that appears earlier than expected that originates from an ectopic focus in the ventricles.
A.premature ventricular contraction   B.heart rate   C.sinus node   D.left coronary artery

© 2017 Network4Learning, Inc.

17. ____ Atrial dysrhythmia; impulse for depolarization originates in 3 or more different foci in the atrium. 3 or more different shaped P waves on ECG.
A.valsalva maneuver   B.electrophysiology   C.sinus arrhythmia   D.multifocal atrial rhythm

18. ____ The act of using equipment to send an electrical shock to the heart to stop an irregular heart rhythm. Defibrillation is the only cure to sudden cardiac arrest.
A.sinus rhythm   B.defibrillation   C.cardiac tamponade   D.palpitation

19. ____ Constriction of the heart that prevent filling of the ventricles. It is usually caused by fluid or blood accumulating in the pericardial sac.
A.thrombolytics   B.cardiac tamponade   C.junctional escape beat   D.holter monitoring

20. ____ Antiarrhythmic infusion for stable wide QRS Tachycardia. Used to treat life-threatening ventricular tachycardia or symptomatic PVC's.
A.ventricular tachycardia   B.sympathetic nervous system   C.procainamide   D.inotropic effect

21. ____ A disruption of the heart rhythm caused by a sudden blunt blow to the chest.
A.electrophysiology   B.commotio cordis   C.intrinsic rate   D.cpr

22. ____ Treats Torsades de Pointes, Ventricular Fibrillation. Electrolyte that causes all muscles to contract. Results in depression early after depolarization.
A.idioventricular rhythm   B.magnesium sulfate   C.sinus node   D.supraventricular tachycardia

23. ____ An unusually large heart. This condition can be a a result of conditions such as an abnormal heart rhythm, stress, or weakening of the heart muscle.
A.lad   B.tropomyosin   C.procainamide   D.enlarged heart

24. ____ Increases force of muscle contraction.
A.intrinsic rate   B.ventricular bigeminy   C.inotropic effect   D.beta blocker

25. ____ Coronary artery that supplies oxygenated blood to the anterior surface of the left ventricle, the ventricular septum, and the papillary muscles of the mitral valve and the bundle of His.
A.sinus node   B.ventricular bigeminy   C.lad   D.cardiac tamponade

26. ____ A series of advanced treatments for cardiac arrest and other life-threatening conditions.
A.cardiac output   B.right coronary artery   C.stent   D.acls

27. ____ Absence of a heartbeat, also known as "flat line". A dire condition in which the heart has no rhythm.
A.mobitz i   B.asystole   C.pr interval   D.vasopressin

28. ____ Originates in the ventricle. Rate is 20-40bpm.
A.idioventricular rhythm   B.left coronary artery   C.supraventricular tachycardia   D.qrs duration

29. ____ At the beginning of contraction, calcium is released and attaches to troponin, allowing cross bridges on the myosin to attach to the actin.
A.congenital heart defect   B.normal sinus rhythm   C.tropomyosin   D.junctional escape beat

30. ____ Pause caused by delay in impulse being initiated in the SA node. pause is < 2 R-R intervals.
A.sinus pause   B.heart rate   C.doppler ultrasound   D.repolarization

31. ____ The normal rate for a given pacemaker cells.
A.algorithm   B.intrinsic rate   C.t wave   D.acls

32. ____ A birth defect of the heart
A.bradycardia   B.inotropic effect   C.congenital heart defect   D.thrombolytics

© 2017 Network4Learning, Inc.

33. ___ A life-saving device that treats sudden cardiac arrest.
A.repolarization B.myocardium C.right ventricle D.aed

34. ___ The amount of time it takes for ventricle depolarization. Measured from when the QRS first leaves the isoelectric line to where the ST segment begins.
A.pericardial effusion B.qrs duration C.thrombolytics D.defibrillation

35. ___ Continuous monitoring of the electrical activity of a patient's heart with a small, portable ECG machine. The device is typically worn around the neck or waist for a 24-hour period.
A.defibrillator B.algorithm C.holter monitoring D.joules

36. ___ High pressure chamber of the heart responsible for pumping oxygenated blood to the systemic circulation.
A.junctional rhythms B.sudden cardiac death C.ventricular tachycardia D.left ventricle

37. ___ Coronary artery that delivers blood to the Right Ventricle, AV junction, and the SA node in 55% of the population.
A.commotio cordis B.doppler ultrasound C.relative refractory period D.right coronary artery

38. ___ A medical device used to treat a victim with a life-threatening irregular heart rhythm.
A.lidocaine action B.supraventricular tachycardia C.junctional tachycardia D.defibrillator

39. ___ A kind of drug that can break up or dissolve clots blocking the flow of blood to the heart muscle. Ideally, the drug should be administered within 90 minutes of being admitted for a heart attack.
A.thrombolytics B.cardiac output C.solatol D.joules

40. ___ Rapid, fluttering heart beats. Heart palpitations can be triggered by exercise, medications, or stress.
A.emergency medical service B.beta blocker C.palpitation D.defibrillation

41. ___ Rate; a positive chronotropic effect would result in an increase in rate
A.chronotropic effect B.first degree block C.idioventricular rhythm D.ventricular septal defect

42. ___ Coronary artery that delivers oxygenated blood to the left side of the heart. Divides into the left anterior descending artery and the circumflex artery.
A.tropomyosin B.right ventricle C.left coronary artery D.bradycardia

43. ___ A PVC that falls on or very near the T wave.
A.emt B.qrs duration C.r on t pvc D.adenosine

44. ___ Slowness of the heart rate, usually less than 60 beats per minute.
A.palpitation B.bradycardia C.repolarization D.junctional escape beat

45. ___ A tube designed to be implanted in a vessel to help keep it open.
A.algorithm B.procainamide C.stent D.intrinsic rate

46. ___ Weak disorganized quivering of the ventricle with no identifying QRS complex.
A.ventricular fibrillation B.lead C.heart rate D.adenosine

47. ___ Tachycardia with rate > 150bpm; no P waves can be identified.
A.pericardial effusion B.lead C.supraventricular tachycardia D.third degree heart block

48. ___ Death as a result of sudden cardiac arrest.
A.supraventricular tachycardia B.sudden cardiac death C.manual defibrillator D.lidocaine action

49. ___ A thin, flexible tube that is inserted into the heart through a peripheral blood vessel to provide therapy and
A.ventricular fibrillation B.catheter C.first degree block D.inferior vena cava

© 2017 Network4Learning, Inc.

50. ____ A rapid, but organized vibration of the heart muscle. Atrial flutter can result in 250-350 heart beats per minute.
A.cardioversion   B.flutter   C.r on t pvc   D.ventricular fibrillation

51. ____ The study of the electrical activity in the heart. Studies and procedures are conducted in the EP Lab of a hospital.
A.idioventricular rhythm   B.algorithm   C.beta blocker   D.electrophysiology

52. ____ Used in stable symptomatic tachycardias that are persistent and do not have wide QRS-Treatment for Afib., and PSVT.
A.premature junctional contraction   B.right atrium   C.calcium channel blocker   D.ventricular fibrillation

53. ____ A wire that conducts electrical current from the defibrillator to the heart. For AEDs, the lead is connected to electrode pads that attach to the patient.
A.cardioversion   B.procainamide   C.left atrium   D.lead

54. ____ A rapid twitching of the heart muscles caused by an abnormal and sometimes chaotic discharge of electrical impulses. Atrial fibrillation results in a rapid and irregular heartbeat.
A.ventricular fibrillation   B.algorithm   C.fibrillation   D.solatol

55. ____ Independent activity of atria and ventricles
A.third degree heart block   B.chronotropic effect   C.sympathetic nervous system   D.inotropic effect

56. ____ One-way valve that allow blood flow from Right Atrium to Right Ventricle.
A.enlarged heart   B.left atrium   C.tricuspid valve   D.doppler ultrasound

57. ____ A congenital heart defect where an abnormal opening in the septum separates the ventricles.
A.relative refractory period   B.right coronary artery   C.intrinsic rate   D.ventricular septal defect

58. ____ Measured from where the P-wave starts to where the QRS first leaves the isoelectric line. Represents atrial depolarization and the delay in the AV node.
A.pr interval   B.valsalva maneuver   C.joules   D.bradycardia

59. ____ Innervates all parts of the heart and all the blood vessels.
A.sympathetic nervous system   B.implantable defibrillator   C.supraventricular tachycardia   D.calcium channel blocker

60. ____ The lower right chamber of the heart that receives deoxygenated blood from the right atrium and pumps it to the lungs through the pulmonary artery.
A.cardiac tamponade   B.right ventricle   C.multifocal atrial rhythm   D.solatol

61. ____ An ECG complex that appears earlier than expected than originates from an ectopic focus in the AV junction.
A.emt   B.premature junctional contraction   C.inferior vena cava   D.intrinsic rate

62. ____ Complex or rhythm that takes over if SA node fails. Beats or rhythm occur after a pause and later than expected.
A.pericardial effusion   B.junctional escape beat   C.cpr   D.r wave

63. ____ The time before the cell is fully repolarized when it can respond to a stimulus.
A.congenital heart defect   B.torsades de pointes   C.relative refractory period   D.sinus node

64. ____ A fast heart rhythm that originates in the ventricles. Also known as V-tach.
A.sympathetic nervous system   B.holter monitoring   C.sinus node   D.ventricular tachycardia

© 2017 Network4Learning, Inc.

65. ____ A forceful attempt at expiration when the airway is closed to stop supraventricular tachycardia.
A.valsalva maneuver   B.pacemaker   C.qrs duration   D.defibrillation

66. ____ An implantable medical device that sends electrical signals to the heart to set the heart rhythm.
A.holter monitoring   B.r wave   C.left ventricle   D.pacemaker

67. ____ An abnormal "whooshing" sound made by blood flowing through the heart.
A.bradycardia   B.heart murmur   C.left atrium   D.fibrillation

68. ____ The number of complete cycles of the contraction and relaxation of the heart muscle per minute. A normal heart rate for adults is 60 to 100 beats per minute.
A.heart rate   B.myocardium   C.solatol   D.left atrium

69. ____ Meets criteria for NSR except rhythm is irregular.
A.sinus arrhythmia   B.algorithm   C.left ventricle   D.palpitation

70. ____ A medical device that is implanted in the body to diagnose and treat abnormal electrical arrhythmias. If an abnormal arrhythmia is detected, the ICD will apply a shock to restore the heart to a normal rhythm.
A.commotio cordis   B.implantable defibrillator   C.valsalva maneuver   D.mobitz i

71. ____ A medical term to describe the normal beating of the heart.
A.endocardium   B.repolarization   C.supraventricular tachycardia   D.sinus rhythm

72. ____ PVC that occurs with every other beat.
A.pulmonary artery   B.congenital heart defect   C.sinus arrhythmia   D.ventricular bigeminy

73. ____ An emergency procedure treating a victim who is unconscious and unresponsive with no signs of circulation.
A.cardiopulmonary resuscitation   B.acls   C.premature ventricular contraction   D.pr interval

74. ____ Large vein that carries deoxygenated blood from the lower venous circulation (below the neck) and empties into the Right Atrium.
A.inferior vena cava   B.tricuspid valve   C.sinus node   D.junctional rhythms

75. ____ An advanced life support medical device that monitors the heart rhythm and allow the user to manually set the energy delivery and deliver a shock.
A.adenosine   B.cardiopulmonary resuscitation   C.tropomyosin   D.manual defibrillator

76. ____ Return of membrane potential to its resting state. K+ move into the cell and Na+ moves out.
A.junctional rhythms   B.sinus rhythm   C.tropomyosin   D.repolarization

77. ____ Fundamental treatment provided to a victim to include CPR and AED use.
A.basic life support   B.congenital heart defect   C.implantable defibrillator   D.right atrium

78. ____ Alternate with epinephrine in patient with pulseless VFib
A.sinus rhythm   B.relative refractory period   C.vasopressin   D.left ventricle

79. ____ Rhythms initiated from impulses that originate from the Atrial Ventricular junction. Intrinsic rate 40-60bpm.
A.sinus rhythm   B.junctional rhythms   C.left ventricular dysfunction   D.congenital heart defect

80. ____ A set of precise rules programmed into a defibrillator to analyze heart rhythms and treat cardiac arrest.
A.algorithm   B.cardiac tamponade   C.supraventricular tachycardia   D.premature ventricular contraction

© 2017 Network4Learning, Inc.

81. ____ Anti-arrhythmic that increases electrical threshold of ventricles during diastole
A.lidocaine action   B.inferior vena cava   C.bradycardia   D.ventricular tachycardia

82. ____ A non-profit organization that establishes the standards in cardiac care.
A.pacemaker   B.inotropic effect   C.congenital heart defect   D.american heart association

83. ____ The 1st positive deflection following the P wave.
A.pericardial effusion   B.r wave   C.sinus pause   D.right atrium

84. ____ A trained and certified professional who can use advanced life support techniques to treat sudden cardiac arrest.
A.t wave   B.ventricular septal defect   C.emt   D.procainamide

85. ____ A four-step process for treating victims of sudden cardiac arrest.
A.pericardial effusion   B. chain of survival   C.basic life support   D.right coronary artery

86. ____ Used in stable symptomatic tachycardia that is persistent and does not have a wide QRS.
A.beta blocker   B.normal sinus rhythm   C.mobitz i   D. chain of survival

87. ____ The upper left chamber of the heart that receives oxygenated blood from the lungs and pumps it to the left ventricle.
A.left atrium   B.electrophysiology   C.r on t pvc   D.ventricular septal defect

88. ____ A condition in which the left ventricle of the heart exhibits decreased functionality. This can lead to heart failure.
A.implantable defibrillator   B.left ventricular dysfunction   C.lead   D.junctional tachycardia

89. ____ A measure of electrical energy equal to the work done when a current of one ampere passes through a resistance of one ohm for one second.
A.joules   B.sinus pause   C.thrombolytics   D.palpitation

90. ____ Junction rhythm with a rate > 100bpm
A.junctional tachycardia   B.holter monitoring   C.right coronary artery   D.procainamide

91. ____ A conduction through the ventricles that results in increase time for ventricular depolarization resulting in a prolonged QRS interval > 0.10 in most leads and > 0.12 in all leads.
A.premature junctional contraction   B.ventricular fibrillation   C.sinus node   D.intraventricular conduction defect

92. ____ Used to treat unstable tachy-arrhythmias if regular and monomorphic; Slows atrial conduction through AV node.
A.qrs duration   B.endocardium   C.right atrium   D.adenosine

93. ____ Inner surface of the heart.
A.emergency medical service   B.endocardium   C.sinus arrhythmia   D.left ventricle

94. ____ Sympathomimetic agent that causes peripheral vasoconstriction (alpha effects) and muscle vasodilation (beta effects).
A.american heart association   B.dopamine   C.cardiac output   D.pulmonary artery

95. ____ polymorphic ventricular tachycardia characterized by QRS complexes that change directions.
A.torsades de pointes   B.sinus pause   C.endocardium   D.sympathetic nervous system

96. ____ A normal heart rate.
A.myocardium   B.pacemaker   C.right ventricle   D.normal sinus rhythm

97. ____ Professional services that respond to 911 calls relating to sudden cardiac arrest.
A.inotropic effect   B.emergency medical service   C.qrs duration   D.adenosine

© 2017 Network4Learning, Inc.

98. ____ An accumulation of fluid in the pericardial sac.
A.heart rate B.pericardial effusion C.beta blocker D.inferior vena cava

99. ____ The amount of blood ejected by the heart in one minute in liters
A.torsades de pointes B. chain of survival C.cardiac output D.junctional tachycardia

100. ____ The most common form of sudden cardiac arrest. A sudden, lethal arrhythmia in which chaotic electrical activity results in the ventricles fluttering rapidly and losing the ability to pump blood.
A. chain of survival B.intraventricular conduction defect C.ventricular fibrillation D.endocardium

From the words provided for each clue, provide the letter of the word which best matches the clue.

101. ____ Anti-arrhythmic that increases electrical threshold of ventricles during diastole
A.bundle of his B.lidocaine action C.thrombolytics D.right ventricle

102. ____ A PVC that falls on or very near the T wave.
A.premature junctional contraction B.ventricular bigeminy C.r on t pvc D.epinephrine

103. ____ Antiarrhythmic infusion for stable wide QRS Tachycardia. Used to treat life-threatening ventricular tachycardia or symptomatic PVC's.
A.mobitz ii B.procainamide C.sudden cardiac death D.atropine

104. ____ Coronary artery that delivers oxygenated blood to the left side of the heart. Divides into the left anterior descending artery and the circumflex artery.
A.bundle of his B.doppler ultrasound C.ablation D.left coronary artery

105. ____ Innervates all parts of the heart and all the blood vessels.
A.right atrium B.sudden cardiac arrest C.sympathetic nervous system D.vasopressin

106. ____ Professional services that respond to 911 calls relating to sudden cardiac arrest.
A.repolarization B.relative refractory period C.emergency medical service D.r on t pvc

107. ____ Rate; a positive chronotropic effect would result in an increase in rate
A.chronotropic effect B.myocardial infarction C.inferior vena cava D.left coronary artery

108. ____ Anti-arrhythmic used to treat atrial-ventricular tachyarrhythmias.
A.pacemaker B.stent C.right coronary artery D.amiodarone

109. ____ The lower right chamber of the heart that receives deoxygenated blood from the right atrium and pumps it to the lungs through the pulmonary artery.
A.right ventricle B.mobitz ii C.emergency medical service D.atrium

110. ____ A form of ultrasound that can detect blood flow. Used to diagnose cardiac disease.
A.right coronary artery B.sudden cardiac arrest C.doppler ultrasound D.atrium

111. ____ The upper left chamber of the heart that receives oxygenated blood from the lungs and pumps it to the left ventricle.
A.left atrium B.biphasic energy C.atrial tachycardia D.pulmonary artery

112. ____ PVC that occurs with every other beat.
A.biphasic energy B.right atrium C.ventricular bigeminy D.procainamide

113. ____ Rhythms initiated from impulses that originate from the Atrial Ventricular junction. Intrinsic rate 40-60bpm.
A.stent B.heart murmur C.r on t pvc D.junctional rhythms

© 2017 Network4Learning, Inc.

114. ____ An abnormal "whooshing" sound made by blood flowing through the heart.
A.repolarization B.procainamide C.heart murmur D.sudden cardiac arrest

115. ____ A kind of drug that can break up or dissolve clots blocking the flow of blood to the heart muscle. Ideally, the drug should be administered within 90 minutes of being admitted for a heart attack.
A.thrombolytics B.lidocaine action C.sudden cardiac death D.pacemaker

116. ____ A heart block where some P waves not conducted through AV node. Some P waves not followed by QRS complexes. P waves that do follow QRS, have consistent intervals.
A.mobitz ii B.left coronary artery C.stent D.repolarization

117. ____ Return of membrane potential to its resting state. K+ move into the cell and Na+ moves out.
A.repolarization B.right ventricle C.procainamide D.atrial tachycardia

118. ____ The time before the cell is fully repolarized when it can respond to a stimulus.
A.relative refractory period B.vasopressin C.premature junctional contraction D.heart rate

119. ____ An accumulation of fluid in the pericardial sac.
A.atrium B.biphasic energy C.pericardial effusion D.sudden cardiac arrest

120. ____ An implantable medical device that sends electrical signals to the heart to set the heart rhythm.
A.ventricular bigeminy B.emergency medical service C.pacemaker D.doppler ultrasound

121. ____ The upper chamber of each half of the heart.
A.chronotropic effect B.junctional rhythms C.atropine D.atrium

122. ____ Alternate with epinephrine in patient with pulseless VFib
A.ablation B.vasopressin C.right ventricle D.atropine

123. ____ A tube designed to be implanted in a vessel to help keep it open.
A.stent B.mobitz ii C.myocardial infarction D.ablation

124. ____ Junction rhythm with a rate > 100bpm
A.sympathetic nervous system B.junctional tachycardia C.pulmonary artery D.atrial tachycardia

125. ____ An ECG complex that appears earlier than expected than originates from an ectopic focus in the AV junction.
A.atrium B.lidocaine action C.premature junctional contraction D.right atrium

126. ____ The sudden, unexpected loss of the heart function, resulting in the loss of effective blood flow.
A.sudden cardiac arrest B.right ventricle C.pacemaker D.left coronary artery

127. ____ The medical term for a heart attack. The blockage or occlusion of a coronary artery causing the loss of blood supply to the heart muscle.
A.ventricular bigeminy B.junctional tachycardia C.relative refractory period D.myocardial infarction

128. ____ Coronary artery that delivers blood to the Right Ventricle, AV junction, and the SA node in 55% of the population.
A.right coronary artery B.pericardial effusion C.thrombolytics D.biphasic energy

129. ____ Conducts impulses from AV node to bundle branches; makes up AV junction
A.bundle of his B.doppler ultrasound C.vasopressin D.heart murmur

130. ____ Pause caused by delay in impulse being initiated in the SA node. pause is < 2 R-R intervals.
A.amiodarone B.ablation C.sinus pause D.heart rate

© 2017 Network4Learning, Inc.

131. ____ A technique to remove or render inactive problematic cardiac tissue.
A.atropine B.ablation C.vasopressin D.heart murmur

132. ____ Sympathomimetic that stimulates alpha, beta 1&2 receptors resulting in cardiac stimulation.
A.chronotropic effect B.sympathetic nervous system C.left atrium D.epinephrine

133. ____ Vessel that delivers blood from the Left Ventricle to Pulmonary veins.
A.repolarization B.epinephrine C.pulmonary artery D.r on t pvc

134. ____ Low pressure cardiac chamber that receives deoxygenated blood from the systemic venous circulation via the inferior vena cava and the superior vena cava.
A.chronotropic effect B.doppler ultrasound C.right atrium D.heart rate

135. ____ Current from a defibrillator is delivered two ways. Biphasic therapy was introduced in the 1990s and lowers the electrical threshold for successful defibrillation.
A.biphasic energy B.atrium C.junctional tachycardia D.sympathetic nervous system

136. ____ Para-sympatholytic that blocks acetylcholine effects on post cholinergic receptors in smooth muscle and SA-AV nodes.
A.sympathetic nervous system B.atropine C.junctional rhythms D.mobitz ii

137. ____ Large vein that carries deoxygenated blood from the lower venous circulation (below the neck) and empties into the Right Atrium.
A.atrium B.amiodarone C.inferior vena cava D.heart rate

138. ____ Death as a result of sudden cardiac arrest.
A.sudden cardiac death B.junctional tachycardia C.sudden cardiac arrest D.pericardial effusion

139. ____ The number of complete cycles of the contraction and relaxation of the heart muscle per minute. A normal heart rate for adults is 60 to 100 beats per minute.
A.repolarization B.ablation C.r on t pvc D.heart rate

140. ____ A rapid heart rhythm resulting in 160-190 beats per minute and is a type of supraventricular tachycardia.
A.procainamide B.relative refractory period C.atrial tachycardia D.right ventricle

© 2017 Network4Learning, Inc.

From the words provided for each clue, provide the letter of the word which best matches the clue.

1. D   Rapid, organized atrial contractions that usually result in a heart rate of 250-350 beats per minute. AF is a form of supraventricular tachycardia.
    A.left coronary artery   B.thrombolytics   C.junctional rhythms   D.atrial flutter

2. D   A form of ultrasound that can detect blood flow. Used to diagnose cardiac disease.
    A.joules   B.inferior vena cava   C.algorithm   D.doppler ultrasound

3. B   Ventricular repolarization; follows the QRS complex.
    A.cardioversion   B.t wave   C.catheter   D.vasopressin

4. C   cardiopulmonary resuscitation.
    A.enlarged heart   B.implantable defibrillator   C.cpr   D.junctional rhythms

5. A   Smooth ridges on the walls of the heart.
    A.trabeculae   B.heart murmur   C.aed   D.third degree heart block

6. A   A rapid rhythm of the heart, with a pulse of 150-250 beats per minute. The condition can last a few minutes or even days. Treatment may come in the form of cardioversion.
    A.supraventricular tachycardia   B.implantable defibrillator   C.third degree heart block   D.solatol

7. B   Vessel that delivers blood from the Left Ventricle to Pulmonary veins.
    A.pacemaker   B.pulmonary artery   C.palpitation   D.cardioversion

8. A   A cluster of cells in the upper right atrium that generates electrical impulses and stimulates the heart to contract and pump blood.
    A.sinus node   B.emt   C.chronotropic effect   D.trabeculae

9. B   A heart block where the PR interval becomes progressively longer until the P wave is not conducted through the ventricle and a QRS complex is dropped.
    A.acls   B.mobitz i   C.flutter   D.electrophysiology

10. C   A medical procedure by which a trained professional converts an abnormally fast heart rate to a normal rate using defibrillation.
    A.inferior vena cava   B.american heart association   C.cardioversion   D.pericardial effusion

11. C   An abnormality or irregularity in the heart rhythm.
    A.chronotropic effect   B.solatol   C.arrhythmia   D.congenital heart defect

12. B   Low pressure cardiac chamber that receives deoxygenated blood from the systemic venous circulation via the inferior vena cava and the superior vena cava.
    A.right coronary artery   B.right atrium   C.sinus pause   D.myocardium

13. B   Normal Sinus Rhythm with PR interval > 0.20.
    A.r on t pvc   B.first degree block   C. chain of survival   D.sudden cardiac death

14. A   Muscle layer of the heart.
    A.myocardium   B.supraventricular tachycardia   C.sinus arrhythmia   D.arrhythmia

15. A   Antiarrythmic infusion for stable wide QRS Tachycardia. Depresses heart rate, slows AV conduction, decreases cardiac output, and lowers systolic and diastolic blood pressure.
    A.solatol   B.premature junctional contraction   C.cpr   D.supraventricular tachycardia

16. A   An ECG complex that appears earlier than expected that originates from an ectopic focus in the ventricles.
    A.premature ventricular contraction   B.heart rate   C.sinus node   D.left coronary artery

© 2017 Network4Learning, Inc.

17. D   Atrial dysrhythmia; impulse for depolarization originates in 3 or more different foci in the atrium. 3 or more different shaped P waves on ECG.
A.valsalva maneuver   B.electrophysiology   C.sinus arrhythmia   D.multifocal atrial rhythm

18. B   The act of using equipment to send an electrical shock to the heart to stop an irregular heart rhythm. Defibrillation is the only cure to sudden cardiac arrest.
A.sinus rhythm   B.defibrillation   C.cardiac tamponade   D.palpitation

19. B   Constriction of the heart that prevent filling of the ventricles. It is usually caused by fluid or blood accumulating in the pericardial sac.
A.thrombolytics   B.cardiac tamponade   C.junctional escape beat   D.holter monitoring

20. C   Antiarrhythmic infusion for stable wide QRS Tachycardia. Used to treat life-threatening ventricular tachycardia or symptomatic PVC's.
A.ventricular tachycardia   B.sympathetic nervous system   C.procainamide   D.inotropic effect

21. B   A disruption of the heart rhythm caused by a sudden blunt blow to the chest.
A.electrophysiology   B.commotio cordis   C.intrinsic rate   D.cpr

22. B   Treats Torsades de Pointes, Ventricular Fibrillation. Electrolyte that causes all muscles to contract. Results in depression early after depolarization.
A.idioventricular rhythm   B.magnesium sulfate   C.sinus node   D.supraventricular tachycardia

23. D   An unusually large heart. This condition can be a a result of conditions such as an abnormal heart rhythm, stress, or weakening of the heart muscle.
A.lad   B.tropomyosin   C.procainamide   D.enlarged heart

24. C   Increases force of muscle contraction.
A.intrinsic rate   B.ventricular bigeminy   C.inotropic effect   D.beta blocker

25. C   Coronary artery that supplies oxygenated blood to the anterior surface of the left ventricle, the ventricular septum, and the papillary muscles of the mitral valve and the bundle of His.
A.sinus node   B.ventricular bigeminy   C.lad   D.cardiac tamponade

26. D   A series of advanced treatments for cardiac arrest and other life-threatening conditions.
A.cardiac output   B.right coronary artery   C.stent   D.acls

27. B   Absence of a heartbeat, also known as "flat line". A dire condition in which the heart has no rhythm.
A.mobitz i   B.asystole   C.pr interval   D.vasopressin

28. A   Originates in the ventricle. Rate is 20-40bpm.
A.idioventricular rhythm   B.left coronary artery   C.supraventricular tachycardia   D.qrs duration

29. C   At the beginning of contraction, calcium is released and attaches to troponin, allowing cross bridges on the myosin to attach to the actin.
A.congenital heart defect   B.normal sinus rhythm   C.tropomyosin   D.junctional escape beat

30. A   Pause caused by delay in impulse being initiated in the SA node. pause is < 2 R-R intervals.
A.sinus pause   B.heart rate   C.doppler ultrasound   D.repolarization

31. B   The normal rate for a given pacemaker cells.
A.algorithm   B.intrinsic rate   C.t wave   D.acls

32. C   A birth defect of the heart
A.bradycardia   B.inotropic effect   C.congenital heart defect   D.thrombolytics

© 2017 Network4Learning, Inc.

33. D A life-saving device that treats sudden cardiac arrest.
A.repolarization B.myocardium C.right ventricle D.aed

34. B The amount of time it takes for ventricle depolarization. Measured from when the QRS first leaves the isoelectric line to where the ST segment begins.
A.pericardial effusion B.qrs duration C.thrombolytics D.defibrillation

35. C Continuous monitoring of the electrical activity of a patient's heart with a small, portable ECG machine. The device is typically worn around the neck or waist for a 24-hour period.
A.defibrillator B.algorithm C.holter monitoring D.joules

36. D High pressure chamber of the heart responsible for pumping oxygenated blood to the systemic circulation.
A.junctional rhythms B.sudden cardiac death C.ventricular tachycardia D.left ventricle

37. D Coronary artery that delivers blood to the Right Ventricle, AV junction, and the SA node in 55% of the population.
A.commotio cordis B.doppler ultrasound C.relative refractory period D.right coronary artery

38. D A medical device used to treat a victim with a life-threatening irregular heart rhythm.
A.lidocaine action B.supraventricular tachycardia C.junctional tachycardia D.defibrillator

39. A A kind of drug that can break up or dissolve clots blocking the flow of blood to the heart muscle. Ideally, the drug should be administered within 90 minutes of being admitted for a heart attack.
A.thrombolytics B.cardiac output C.solatol D.joules

40. C Rapid, fluttering heart beats. Heart palpitations can be triggered by exercise, medications, or stress.
A.emergency medical service B.beta blocker C.palpitation D.defibrillation

41. A Rate; a positive chronotropic effect would result in an increase in rate
A.chronotropic effect B.first degree block C.idioventricular rhythm D.ventricular septal defect

42. C Coronary artery that delivers oxygenated blood to the left side of the heart. Divides into the left anterior descending artery and the circumflex artery.
A.tropomyosin B.right ventricle C.left coronary artery D.bradycardia

43. C A PVC that falls on or very near the T wave.
A.emt B.qrs duration C.r on t pvc D.adenosine

44. B Slowness of the heart rate, usually less than 60 beats per minute.
A.palpitation B.bradycardia C.repolarization D.junctional escape beat

45. C A tube designed to be implanted in a vessel to help keep it open.
A.algorithm B.procainamide C.stent D.intrinsic rate

46. A Weak disorganized quivering of the ventricle with no identifying QRS complex.
A.ventricular fibrillation B.lead C.heart rate D.adenosine

47. C Tachycardia with rate > 150bpm; no P waves can be identified.
A.pericardial effusion B.lead C.supraventricular tachycardia D.third degree heart block

48. B Death as a result of sudden cardiac arrest.
A.supraventricular tachycardia B.sudden cardiac death C.manual defibrillator D.lidocaine action

49. B A thin, flexible tube that is inserted into the heart through a peripheral blood vessel to provide therapy and
A.ventricular fibrillation B.catheter C.first degree block D.inferior vena cava

© 2017 Network4Learning, Inc.

50. B A rapid, but organized vibration of the heart muscle. Atrial flutter can result in 250-350 heart beats per minute.
A.cardioversion   B.flutter   C.r on t pvc   D.ventricular fibrillation

51. D The study of the electrical activity in the heart. Studies and procedures are conducted in the EP Lab of a hospital.
A.idioventricular rhythm   B.algorithm   C.beta blocker   D.electrophysiology

52. C Used in stable symptomatic tachycardias that are persistent and do not have wide QRS-Treatment for Afib., and PSVT.
A.premature junctional contraction   B.right atrium   C.calcium channel blocker   D.ventricular fibrillation

53. D A wire that conducts electrical current from the defibrillator to the heart. For AEDs, the lead is connected to electrode pads that attach to the patient.
A.cardioversion   B.procainamide   C.left atrium   D.lead

54. C A rapid twitching of the heart muscles caused by an abnormal and sometimes chaotic discharge of electrical impulses. Atrial fibrillation results in a rapid and irregular heartbeat.
A.ventricular fibrillation   B.algorithm   C.fibrillation   D.solatol

55. A Independent activity of atria and ventricles
A.third degree heart block   B.chronotropic effect   C.sympathetic nervous system   D.inotropic effect

56. C One-way valve that allow blood flow from Right Atrium to Right Ventricle.
A.enlarged heart   B.left atrium   C.tricuspid valve   D.doppler ultrasound

57. D A congenital heart defect where an abnormal opening in the septum separates the ventricles.
A.relative refractory period   B.right coronary artery   C.intrinsic rate   D.ventricular septal defect

58. A Measured from where the P-wave starts to where the QRS first leaves the isoelectric line. Represents atrial depolarization and the delay in the AV node.
A.pr interval   B.valsalva maneuver   C.joules   D.bradycardia

59. A Innervates all parts of the heart and all the blood vessels.
A.sympathetic nervous system   B.implantable defibrillator   C.supraventricular tachycardia   D.calcium channel blocker

60. B The lower right chamber of the heart that receives deoxygenated blood from the right atrium and pumps it to the lungs through the pulmonary artery.
A.cardiac tamponade   B.right ventricle   C.multifocal atrial rhythm   D.solatol

61. B An ECG complex that appears earlier than expected than originates from an ectopic focus in the AV junction.
A.emt   B.premature junctional contraction   C.inferior vena cava   D.intrinsic rate

62. B Complex or rhythm that takes over if SA node fails. Beats or rhythm occur after a pause and later than expected.
A.pericardial effusion   B.junctional escape beat   C.cpr   D.r wave

63. C The time before the cell is fully repolarized when it can respond to a stimulus.
A.congenital heart defect   B.torsades de pointes   C.relative refractory period   D.sinus node

64. D A fast heart rhythm that originates in the ventricles. Also known as V-tach.
A.sympathetic nervous system   B.holter monitoring   C.sinus node   D.ventricular tachycardia

© 2017 Network4Learning, Inc.

65. A   A forceful attempt at expiration when the airway is closed to stop supraventricular tachycardia.
    A.valsalva maneuver   B.pacemaker   C.qrs duration   D.defibrillation

66. D   An implantable medical device that sends electrical signals to the heart to set the heart rhythm.
    A.holter monitoring   B.r wave   C.left ventricle   D.pacemaker

67. B   An abnormal "whooshing" sound made by blood flowing through the heart.
    A.bradycardia   B.heart murmur   C.left atrium   D.fibrillation

68. A   The number of complete cycles of the contraction and relaxation of the heart muscle per minute. A normal heart rate for adults is 60 to 100 beats per minute.
    A.heart rate   B.myocardium   C.solatol   D.left atrium

69. A   Meets criteria for NSR except rhythm is irregular.
    A.sinus arrhythmia   B.algorithm   C.left ventricle   D.palpitation

70. B   A medical device that is implanted in the body to diagnose and treat abnormal electrical arrhythmias. If an abnormal arrhythmia is detected, the ICD will apply a shock to restore the heart to a normal rhythm.
    A.commotio cordis   B.implantable defibrillator   C.valsalva maneuver   D.mobitz i

71. D   A medical term to describe the normal beating of the heart.
    A.endocardium   B.repolarization   C.supraventricular tachycardia   D.sinus rhythm

72. D   PVC that occurs with every other beat.
    A.pulmonary artery   B.congenital heart defect   C.sinus arrhythmia   D.ventricular bigeminy

73. A   An emergency procedure treating a victim who is unconscious and unresponsive with no signs of circulation.
    A.cardiopulmonary resuscitation   B.acls   C.premature ventricular contraction   D.pr interval

74. A   Large vein that carries deoxygenated blood from the lower venous circulation (below the neck) and empties into the Right Atrium.
    A.inferior vena cava   B.tricuspid valve   C.sinus node   D.junctional rhythms

75. D   An advanced life support medical device that monitors the heart rhythm and allow the user to manually set the energy delivery and deliver a shock.
    A.adenosine   B.cardiopulmonary resuscitation   C.tropomyosin   D.manual defibrillator

76. D   Return of membrane potential to its resting state. K+ move into the cell and Na+ moves out.
    A.junctional rhythms   B.sinus rhythm   C.tropomyosin   D.repolarization

77. A   Fundamental treatment provided to a victim to include CPR and AED use.
    A.basic life support   B.congenital heart defect   C.implantable defibrillator   D.right atrium

78. C   Alternate with epinephrine in patient with pulseless VFib
    A.sinus rhythm   B.relative refractory period   C.vasopressin   D.left ventricle

79. B   Rhythms initiated from impulses that originate from the Atrial Ventricular junction. Intrinsic rate 40-60bpm.
    A.sinus rhythm   B.junctional rhythms   C.left ventricular dysfunction   D.congenital heart defect

80. A   A set of precise rules programmed into a defibrillator to analyze heart rhythms and treat cardiac arrest.
    A.algorithm   B.cardiac tamponade   C.supraventricular tachycardia   D.premature ventricular contraction

© 2017 Network4Learning, Inc.

81. A Anti-arrhythmic that increases electrical threshold of ventricles during diastole
    A.lidocaine action B.inferior vena cava C.bradycardia D.ventricular tachycardia

82. D A non-profit organization that establishes the standards in cardiac care.
    A.pacemaker B.inotropic effect C.congenital heart defect D.american heart association

83. B The 1st positive deflection following the P wave.
    A.pericardial effusion B.r wave C.sinus pause D.right atrium

84. C A trained and certified professional who can use advanced life support techniques to treat sudden cardiac arrest.
    A.t wave B.ventricular septal defect C.emt D.procainamide

85. B A four-step process for treating victims of sudden cardiac arrest.
    A.pericardial effusion B. chain of survival C.basic life support D.right coronary artery

86. A Used in stable symptomatic tachycardia that is persistent and does not have a wide QRS.
    A.beta blocker B.normal sinus rhythm C.mobitz i D. chain of survival

87. A The upper left chamber of the heart that receives oxygenated blood from the lungs and pumps it to the left ventricle.
    A.left atrium B.electrophysiology C.r on t pvc D.ventricular septal defect

88. B A condition in which the left ventricle of the heart exhibits decreased functionality. This can lead to heart failure.
    A.implantable defibrillator B.left ventricular dysfunction C.lead D.junctional tachycardia

89. A A measure of electrical energy equal to the work done when a current of one ampere passes through a resistance of one ohm for one second.
    A.joules B.sinus pause C.thrombolytics D.palpitation

90. A Junction rhythm with a rate > 100bpm
    A.junctional tachycardia B.holter monitoring C.right coronary artery D.procainamide

91. D A conduction through the ventricles that results in increase time for ventricular depolarization resulting in a prolonged QRS interval > 0.10 in most leads and > 0.12 in all leads.
    A.premature junctional contraction B.ventricular fibrillation C.sinus node D.intraventricular conduction defect

92. D Used to treat unstable tachy-arrhythmias if regular and monomorphic; Slows atrial conduction through AV node.
    A.qrs duration B.endocardium C.right atrium D.adenosine

93. B Inner surface of the heart.
    A.emergency medical service B.endocardium C.sinus arrhythmia D.left ventricle

94. B Sympathomimetic agent that causes peripheral vasoconstriction (alpha effects) and muscle vasodilation (beta effects).
    A.american heart association B.dopamine C.cardiac output D.pulmonary artery

95. A polymorphic ventricular tachycardia characterized by QRS complexes that change directions.
    A.torsades de pointes B.sinus pause C.endocardium D.sympathetic nervous system

96. D A normal heart rate.
    A.myocardium B.pacemaker C.right ventricle D.normal sinus rhythm

97. B Professional services that respond to 911 calls relating to sudden cardiac arrest.
    A.inotropic effect B.emergency medical service C.qrs duration D.adenosine

© 2017 Network4Learning, Inc.

98. B   An accumulation of fluid in the pericardial sac.
        A.heart rate   B.pericardial effusion   C.beta blocker   D.inferior vena cava

99. C   The amount of blood ejected by the heart in one minute in liters
        A.torsades de pointes   B. chain of survival   C.cardiac output   D.junctional tachycardia

100. C The most common form of sudden cardiac arrest. A sudden, lethal arrhythmia in which chaotic
        electrical activity results in the ventricles fluttering rapidly and losing the ability to pump blood.
        A. chain of survival   B.intraventricular conduction defect   C.ventricular fibrillation   D.endocardium

From the words provided for each clue, provide the letter of the word which best matches the clue.

101. B Anti-arrhythmic that increases electrical threshold of ventricles during diastole
        A.bundle of his   B.lidocaine action   C.thrombolytics   D.right ventricle

102. C A PVC that falls on or very near the T wave.
        A.premature junctional contraction   B.ventricular bigeminy   C.r on t pvc   D.epinephrine

103. B Antiarrhythmic infusion for stable wide QRS Tachycardia. Used to treat life-threatening ventricular
        tachycardia or symptomatic PVC's.
        A.mobitz ii   B.procainamide   C.sudden cardiac death   D.atropine

104. D Coronary artery that delivers oxygenated blood to the left side of the heart. Divides into the left
        anterior descending artery and the circumflex artery.
        A.bundle of his   B.doppler ultrasound   C.ablation   D.left coronary artery

105. C Innervates all parts of the heart and all the blood vessels.
        A.right atrium   B.sudden cardiac arrest   C.sympathetic nervous system   D.vasopressin

106. C Professional services that respond to 911 calls relating to sudden cardiac arrest.
        A.repolarization   B.relative refractory period   C.emergency medical service   D.r on t pvc

107. A Rate; a positive chronotropic effect would result in an increase in rate
        A.chronotropic effect   B.myocardial infarction   C.inferior vena cava   D.left coronary artery

108. D Anti-arrhythmic used to treat atrial-ventricular tachyarrhythmias.
        A.pacemaker   B.stent   C.right coronary artery   D.amiodarone

109. A The lower right chamber of the heart that receives deoxygenated blood from the right atrium and
        pumps it to the lungs through the pulmonary artery.
        A.right ventricle   B.mobitz ii   C.emergency medical service   D.atrium

110. C A form of ultrasound that can detect blood flow. Used to diagnose cardiac disease.
        A.right coronary artery   B.sudden cardiac arrest   C.doppler ultrasound   D.atrium

111. A The upper left chamber of the heart that receives oxygenated blood from the lungs and pumps it to
        the left ventricle.
        A.left atrium   B.biphasic energy   C.atrial tachycardia   D.pulmonary artery

112. C PVC that occurs with every other beat.
        A.biphasic energy   B.right atrium   C.ventricular bigeminy   D.procainamide

113. D Rhythms initiated from impulses that originate from the Atrial Ventricular junction. Intrinsic rate 40-
        60bpm.
        A.stent   B.heart murmur   C.r on t pvc   D.junctional rhythms

© 2017 Network4Learning, Inc.

114. C   An abnormal "whooshing" sound made by blood flowing through the heart.
      A.repolarization B.procainamide C.heart murmur D.sudden cardiac arrest

115. A   A kind of drug that can break up or dissolve clots blocking the flow of blood to the heart muscle. Ideally, the drug should be administered within 90 minutes of being admitted for a heart attack.
      A.thrombolytics B.lidocaine action C.sudden cardiac death D.pacemaker

116. A   A heart block where some P waves not conducted through AV node. Some P waves not followed by QRS complexes. P waves that do follow QRS, have consistent intervals.
      A.mobitz ii B.left coronary artery C.stent D.repolarization

117. A   Return of membrane potential to its resting state. K+ move into the cell and Na+ moves out.
      A.repolarization B.right ventricle C.procainamide D.atrial tachycardia

118. A   The time before the cell is fully repolarized when it can respond to a stimulus.
      A.relative refractory period B.vasopressin C.premature junctional contraction D.heart rate

119. C   An accumulation of fluid in the pericardial sac.
      A.atrium B.biphasic energy C.pericardial effusion D.sudden cardiac arrest

120. C   An implantable medical device that sends electrical signals to the heart to set the heart rhythm.
      A.ventricular bigeminy B.emergency medical service C.pacemaker D.doppler ultrasound

121. D   The upper chamber of each half of the heart.
      A.chronotropic effect B.junctional rhythms C.atropine D.atrium

122. B   Alternate with epinephrine in patient with pulseless VFib
      A.ablation B.vasopressin C.right ventricle D.atropine

123. A   A tube designed to be implanted in a vessel to help keep it open.
      A.stent B.mobitz ii C.myocardial infarction D.ablation

124. B   Junction rhythm with a rate > 100bpm
      A.sympathetic nervous system B.junctional tachycardia C.pulmonary artery D.atrial tachycardia

125. C   An ECG complex that appears earlier than expected than originates from an ectopic focus in the AV junction.
      A.atrium B.lidocaine action C.premature junctional contraction D.right atrium

126. A   The sudden, unexpected loss of the heart function, resulting in the loss of effective blood flow.
      A.sudden cardiac arrest B.right ventricle C.pacemaker D.left coronary artery

127. D   The medical term for a heart attack. The blockage or occlusion of a coronary artery causing the loss of blood supply to the heart muscle.
      A.ventricular bigeminy B.junctional tachycardia C.relative refractory period D.myocardial infarction

128. A   Coronary artery that delivers blood to the Right Ventricle, AV junction, and the SA node in 55% of the population.
      A.right coronary artery B.pericardial effusion C.thrombolytics D.biphasic energy

129. A   Conducts impulses from AV node to bundle branches; makes up AV junction
      A.bundle of his B.doppler ultrasound C.vasopressin D.heart murmur

130. C   Pause caused by delay in impulse being initiated in the SA node. pause is < 2 R-R intervals.
      A.amiodarone B.ablation C.sinus pause D.heart rate

© 2017 Network4Learning, Inc.

131. B   A technique to remove or render inactive problematic cardiac tissue.
       A.atropine   B.ablation   C.vasopressin   D.heart murmur

132. D   Sympathomimetic that stimulates alpha, beta 1&2 receptors resulting in cardiac stimulation.
       A.chronotropic effect   B.sympathetic nervous system   C.left atrium   D.epinephrine

133. C   Vessel that delivers blood from the Left Ventricle to Pulmonary veins.
       A.repolarization   B.epinephrine   C.pulmonary artery   D.r on t pvc

134. C   Low pressure cardiac chamber that receives deoxygenated blood from the systemic venous
       circulation via the inferior vena cava and the superior vena cava.
       A.chronotropic effect   B.doppler ultrasound   C.right atrium   D.heart rate

135. A   Current from a defibrillator is delivered two ways. Biphasic therapy was introduced in the 1990s
       and lowers the electrical threshold for successful defibrillation.
       A.biphasic energy   B.atrium   C.junctional tachycardia   D.sympathetic nervous system

136. B   Para-sympatholytic that blocks acetylcholine effects on post cholinergic receptors in smooth
       muscle and SA-AV nodes.
       A.sympathetic nervous system   B.atropine   C.junctional rhythms   D.mobitz ii

137. C   Large vein that carries deoxygenated blood from the lower venous circulation (below the neck) and
       empties into the Right Atrium.
       A.atrium   B.amiodarone   C.inferior vena cava   D.heart rate

138. A   Death as a result of sudden cardiac arrest.
       A.sudden cardiac death   B.junctional tachycardia   C.sudden cardiac arrest   D.pericardial effusion

139. D   The number of complete cycles of the contraction and relaxation of the heart muscle per minute. A
       normal heart rate for adults is 60 to 100 beats per minute.
       A.repolarization   B.ablation   C.r on t pvc   D.heart rate

140. C   A rapid heart rhythm resulting in 160-190 beats per minute and is a type of supraventricular
       tachycardia.
       A.procainamide   B.relative refractory period   C.atrial tachycardia   D.right ventricle

© 2017 Network4Learning, Inc.

Matching

Provide the word that best matches each clue.

1. _____ The upper left chamber of the heart that receives oxygenated blood from the lungs and pumps it to the left ventricle.

2. _____ Normal Sinus Rhythm with PR interval > 0.20.

3. _____ A series of advanced treatments for cardiac arrest and other life-threatening conditions.

4. _____ Smooth ridges on the walls of the heart.

5. _____ A rapid heart rhythm resulting in 160-190 beats per minute and is a type of supraventricular tachycardia.

6. _____ One-way valve that allow blood flow from the Left Atrium to the Left Ventricle and prevents blood from flowing back to the LA during Ventricular systole.

7. _____ Anti-arrhythmic that increases electrical threshold of ventricles during diastole

8. _____ One-way valve between low pressure Right Ventricle and low pressure Pulmonary artery. Allows blood flow from Right Ventricle to Pulmonary Artery and prevents blood from flowing back to RV during vent. diastole.

9. _____ Innervates all parts of the heart and all the blood vessels.

10. _____ Absence of a heartbeat, also known as "flat line". A dire condition in which the heart has no rhythm.

11. _____ The act of using equipment to send an electrical shock to the heart to stop an irregular heart rhythm. Defibrillation is the only cure to sudden cardiac arrest.

12. _____ A test that measures and records the electrical activity in the heart.

© 2017 Network4Learning, Inc.

13. _____ Used in stable symptomatic tachycardia that is persistent and does not have a wide QRS.

14. _____ A birth defect of the heart

15. _____ polymorphic ventricular tachycardia characterized by QRS complexes that change directions.

16. _____ An ECG complex that appears earlier than expected than originates from an ectopic focus in the AV junction.

17. _____ An advanced life support medical device that monitors the heart rhythm and allow the user to manually set the energy delivery and deliver a shock.

18. _____ A rapid twitching of the heart muscles caused by an abnormal and sometimes chaotic discharge of electrical impulses. Atrial fibrillation results in a rapid and irregular heartbeat.

19. _____ Coronary artery that delivers blood to the Right Ventricle, AV junction, and the SA node in 55% of the population.

20. _____ Large vein that carries deoxygenated blood from the lower venous circulation (below the neck) and empties into the Right Atrium.

21. _____ A thin, flexible tube that is inserted into the heart through a peripheral blood vessel to provide therapy and

22. _____ The number of complete cycles of the contraction and relaxation of the heart muscle per minute. A normal heart rate for adults is 60 to 100 beats per minute.

23. _____ At the beginning of contraction, calcium is released and attaches to troponin, allowing cross bridges on the myosin to attach to the actin.

24. _____ Junction rhythm with a rate > 100bpm

© 2017 Network4Learning, Inc.

25. _____   A set of precise rules programmed into a defibrillator to analyze heart rhythms and treat cardiac arrest.

26. _____   Primary pacemaker of the heart. The intrinsic rate of the SA node is 60-100 bpm

A. Fibrillation
C. Heart Rate
E. Junctional Tachycardia
G. Asystole
I. Electrocardiogram
K. Torsades de Pointes
M. Sympathetic Nervous System
O. Beta blocker
Q. Lidocaine action
S. Defibrillation
U. Algorithm
W. Catheter
Y. First degree block

B. SA Node
D. Pulmonary Valve
F. Right Coronary Artery
H. Tropomyosin
J. Atrial Tachycardia
L. Inferior Vena Cava
N. ACLS
P. Premature Junctional Contraction
R. Congenital Heart Defect
T. Trabeculae
V. Left Atrium
X. Manual Defibrillator
Z. Mitral Valve

Provide the word that best matches each clue.

27. _____   A tube designed to be implanted in a vessel to help keep it open.

28. _____   Low pressure chamber that receives oxygenated blood from the pulmonary system via the pulmonary veins.

29. _____   Used for heart block and ventricular arrhythmias. A sympathomimetic that results in pronounced stimulation of beta1 & beta2 receptors of heart and bronchi.

30. _____   Alternate with epinephrine in patient with pulseless VFib

31. _____   Absence of a heartbeat, also known as "flat line". A dire condition in which the heart has no rhythm.

32. _____   The time before the cell is fully repolarized when it can respond to a stimulus.

33. _____   The lower right chamber of the heart that receives deoxygenated blood from the right atrium and pumps it to the lungs through the pulmonary artery.

© 2017 Network4Learning, Inc.

34. _____ Rhythms initiated from impulses that originate from the Atrial Ventricular junction. Intrinsic rate 40-60bpm.

35. _____ Impulse for ventricular contraction originated from ventricle with a rate of > 100pbm.

36. _____ Conducts impulses from AV node to bundle branches; makes up AV junction

37. _____ Innervates all parts of the heart and all the blood vessels.

38. _____ Large vein that carries deoxygenated blood from the lower venous circulation (below the neck) and empties into the Right Atrium.

39. _____ A medical procedure by which a trained professional converts an abnormally fast heart rate to a normal rate using defibrillation.

40. _____ The sudden, unexpected loss of the heart function, resulting in the loss of effective blood flow.

41. _____ Measured from where the P-wave starts to where the QRS first leaves the isoelectric line. Represents atrial depolarization and the delay in the AV node.

42. _____ Outer surface of the heart.

43. _____ Junction rhythm with a rate > 100bpm

44. _____ Part of the ECG complex that reflects atrial depolarization.

45. _____ An emergency procedure treating a victim who is unconscious and unresponsive with no signs of circulation.

46. _____ Sympathomimetic that stimulates alpha, beta 1&2 receptors resulting in cardiac stimulation.

47. _____ The first negative deflection following the P wave.

48. _____ High pressure chamber of the heart responsible for pumping oxygenated blood to the systemic circulation.

© 2017 Network4Learning, Inc.

49. _____ Current from a defibrillator is delivered two ways. Biphasic therapy was introduced in the 1990s and lowers the electrical threshold for successful defibrillation.

50. _____ A fast heart rhythm that originates in the ventricles. Also known as V-tach.

51. _____ Coronary artery that delivers blood to the Right Ventricle, AV junction, and the SA node in 55% of the population.

52. _____ A rapid rhythm of the heart, with a pulse of 150-250 beats per minute. The condition can last a few minutes or even days. Treatment may come in the form of cardioversion.

A. Epicardium
C. Cardioversion
E. Vasopressin
G. Bundle of His
I. Ventricular Tachycardia
K. Biphasic Energy
M. Epinephrine
O. Supraventricular Tachycardia
Q. Cardiopulmonary Resuscitation
S. Left Atrium
U. Right Coronary Artery
W. Stent
Y. Junctional Tachycardia

B. Relative Refractory Period
D. Sudden Cardiac Arrest
F. Right Ventricle
H. Inferior Vena Cava
J. Asystole
L. PR interval
N. Junctional Rhythms
P. Isuprel
R. Sympathetic Nervous System
T. Ventricular Tachycardia
V. Q wave
X. Left Ventricle
Z. P Wave

Provide the word that best matches each clue.

53. _____ Sympathomimetic agent that causes peripheral vasoconstriction (alpha effects) and muscle vasodilation (beta effects).

54. _____ The most common form of sudden cardiac arrest. A sudden, lethal arrhythmia in which chaotic electrical activity results in the ventricles fluttering rapidly and losing the ability to pump blood.

55. _____ Low pressure chamber that receives oxygenated blood from the pulmonary system via the pulmonary veins.

56. _____ A form of ultrasound that can detect blood flow. Used to diagnose cardiac disease.

© 2017 Network4Learning, Inc.

57. _____ A technique to remove or render inactive problematic cardiac tissue.

58. _____ Treats Torsades de Pointes, Ventricular Fibrillation. Electrolyte that causes all muscles to contract. Results in depression early after depolarization.

59. _____ A four-step process for treating victims of sudden cardiac arrest.

60. _____ The upper chamber of each half of the heart.

61. _____ An unusually large heart. This condition can be a a result of conditions such as an abnormal heart rhythm, stress, or weakening of the heart muscle.

62. _____ An emergency procedure treating a victim who is unconscious and unresponsive with no signs of circulation.

63. _____ cardiopulmonary resuscitation.

64. _____ Used for heart block and ventricular arrhythmias. A sympathomimetic that results in pronounced stimulation of beta1 & beta2 receptors of heart and bronchi.

65. _____ The sudden, unexpected loss of the heart function, resulting in the loss of effective blood flow.

66. _____ Part of the ECG complex that reflects atrial depolarization.

67. _____ A measure of electrical energy equal to the work done when a current of one ampere passes through a resistance of one ohm for one second.

68. _____ Medulla and mediated by vagus nerve; slows Heart Rate, decreases speed of conduction through AV node, slight depression in contractility.

69. _____ Constriction of the heart that prevent filling of the ventricles. It is usually caused by fluid or blood accumulating in the pericardial sac.

© 2017 Network4Learning, Inc.

70. _____ Alternate with epinephrine in patient with pulseless VFib

71. _____ Measured from where the P-wave starts to where the QRS first leaves the isoelectric line. Represents atrial depolarization and the delay in the AV node.

72. _____ The act of using equipment to send an electrical shock to the heart to stop an irregular heart rhythm. Defibrillation is the only cure to sudden cardiac arrest.

73. _____ Amount of blood ejected with each ventricular contraction.

74. _____ The time before the cell is fully repolarized when it can respond to a stimulus.

75. _____ The amount of blood ejected by the heart in one minute in liters

76. _____ Used in stable symptomatic tachycardia that is persistent and does not have a wide QRS.

77. _____ Caused by stimulation of para-sympathetic Nervous System and results in slowing of the Heart Rate. Can be initiated intentionally with carotid massage or valsalva maneuver.

78. _____ Coronary artery that supplies oxygenated blood to the anterior surface of the left ventricle, the ventricular septum, and the papillary muscles of the mitral valve and the bundle of His.

A. Stroke Volume
B. Left Atrium
C. Ventricular Fibrillation
D. Vasovagal Response
E. Magnesium sulfate
F. Cardiac Tamponade
G. Sudden Cardiac Arrest
H. P Wave
I. Chain of Survival
J. Cardiopulmonary Resuscitation
K. Ablation
L. Doppler Ultrasound
M. PR interval
N. Relative Refractory Period
O. Cardiac Output
P. Dopamine
Q. Parasympathetic Nervous System
R. CPR
S. Vasopressin
T. Joules
U. Isuprel
V. LAD
W. Enlarged Heart
X. Defibrillation
Y. Beta blocker
Z. Atrium

© 2017 Network4Learning, Inc.

Provide the word that best matches each clue.

79. _____ PVC that occurs with every other beat.

80. _____ Atrial tachycardia that starts and stops suddenly.

81. _____ Anti-arrhythmic used to treat atrial-ventricular tachyarrhythmias.

82. _____ A life-saving device that treats sudden cardiac arrest.

83. _____ The medical term for a heart attack. The blockage or occlusion of a coronary artery causing the loss of blood supply to the heart muscle.

84. _____ Originates in the ventricle. Rate is 20-40bpm.

85. _____ Rhythms initiated from impulses that originate from the Atrial Ventricular junction. Intrinsic rate 40-60bpm.

86. _____ Return of membrane potential to its resting state. K+ move into the cell and Na+ moves out.

87. _____ An ECG complex that appears earlier than expected than originates from an ectopic focus in the AV junction.

88. _____ An abnormal, very fast and disorganized heart rate with chaotic electrical activity in the atria of the heart.

89. _____ An abnormality or irregularity in the heart rhythm.

90. _____ A measure of electrical energy equal to the work done when a current of one ampere passes through a resistance of one ohm for one second.

91. _____ A forceful attempt at expiration when the airway is closed to stop supraventricular tachycardia.

92. _____ Alternate with epinephrine in patient with pulseless VFib

© 2017 Network4Learning, Inc.

93. _____ A rapid heart rhythm resulting in 160-190 beats per minute and is a type of supraventricular tachycardia.

94. _____ A heart block where some P waves not conducted through AV node. Some P waves not followed by QRS complexes. P waves that do follow QRS, have consistent intervals.

95. _____ Anti-arrhythmic that increases electrical threshold of ventricles during diastole

96. _____ Smooth ridges on the walls of the heart.

97. _____ Conducts impulses from AV node to bundle branches; makes up AV junction

98. _____ Para-sympatholytic that blocks acetylcholine effects on post cholinergic receptors in smooth muscle and SA-AV nodes.

99. _____ A pause caused by the SA node not firing; pause measures more than 2 R-R intervals.

100. _____ At the beginning of contraction, calcium is released and attaches to troponin, allowing cross bridges on the myosin to attach to the actin.

101. _____ A rapid heart rate, usually over 100 beats per minute.

102. _____ A series of advanced treatments for cardiac arrest and other life-threatening conditions.

103. _____ The lower left chamber of the heart that receives oxygenated blood from the left atrium and pumps the blood through the aorta to the body.

104. _____ A condition in which the left ventricle of the heart exhibits decreased functionality. This can lead to heart failure.

A. Vasopressin
C. Trabeculae
E. Mobitz II

B. Left Ventricular Dysfunction
D. Sinus Arrest
F. Premature Junctional Contraction

© 2017 Network4Learning, Inc.

G. Repolarization
I. Paroxysmal Atrial Tachycardia
K. Valsalva Maneuver
M. Joules
O. ACLS
Q. Atrial Tachycardia
S. Bundle of His
U. Tachycardia
W. Left Ventricle
Y. Atropine

H. AED
J. Myocardial Infarction
L. Lidocaine action
N. Ventricular Bigeminy
P. Junctional Rhythms
R. Idioventricular Rhythm
T. Tropomyosin
V. Arrhythmia
X. Amiodarone
Z. Atrial Fibrillation

Provide the word that best matches each clue.

105.	_____	PVC that occurs with every other beat.
106.	_____	Impulse for ventricular contraction originated from ventricle with a rate of > 100pbm.
107.	_____	A series of advanced treatments for cardiac arrest and other life-threatening conditions.
108.	_____	Anti-arrhythmic used to treat atrial-ventricular tachyarrhythmias.
109.	_____	An ECG complex that appears earlier than expected that originates from an ectopic focus in the ventricles.
110.	_____	Innervates all parts of the heart and all the blood vessels.
111.	_____	Immunity protection provided by each state government and the Federal government to encourage lay responders to treat a victim of sudden cardiac arrest with an AED and CPR.
112.	_____	Antiarrhythmic infusion for stable wide QRS Tachycardia. Used to treat life-threatening ventricular tachycardia or symptomatic PVC's.
113.	_____	A life-saving device that treats sudden cardiac arrest.

© 2017 Network4Learning, Inc.

114. _____ Coronary artery that supplies oxygenated blood to the anterior surface of the left ventricle, the ventricular septum, and the papillary muscles of the mitral valve and the bundle of His.

115. _____ A thin, flexible tube that is inserted into the heart through a peripheral blood vessel to provide therapy and

116. _____ Independent activity of atria and ventricles

117. _____ Death as a result of sudden cardiac arrest.

118. _____ The normal rate for a given pacemaker cells.

119. _____ Pause when impulse not conducted out of SA node; pause is exactly 2 R-R intervals.

120. _____ Vessel that delivers blood from the Left Ventricle to Pulmonary veins.

121. _____ A rapid heart rate, usually over 100 beats per minute.

122. _____ A heart block where the PR interval becomes progressively longer until the P wave is not conducted through the ventricle and a QRS complex is dropped.

123. _____ A medical term to describe the normal beating of the heart.

124. _____ One-way valve that allow blood flow from Right Atrium to Right Ventricle.

125. _____ Used in stable symptomatic tachycardia that is persistent and does not have a wide QRS.

126. _____ Alternate with epinephrine in patient with pulseless VFib

© 2017 Network4Learning, Inc.

127. _____ Constriction of the heart that prevent filling of the ventricles. It is usually caused by fluid or blood accumulating in the pericardial sac.

128. _____ Increases force of muscle contraction.

129. _____ Used in stable symptomatic tachycardias that are persistent and do not have wide QRS-Treatment for Afib., and PSVT.

130. _____ A medical device that is implanted in the body to diagnose and treat abnormal electrical arrhythmias. If an abnormal arrhythmia is detected, the ICD will apply a shock to restore the heart to a normal rhythm.

A. Amiodarone
C. ACLS
E. Ventricular Bigeminy
G. Calcium channel blocker
I. Cardiac Tamponade
K. Sinus Exit Block
M. Vasopressin
O. Mobitz I
Q. Sudden Cardiac Death
S. Intrinsic Rate
U. AED
W. Procainamide
Y. Inotropic Effect

B. Premature Ventricular Contraction
D. Ventricular Tachycardia
F. Sinus Rhythm
H. Tricuspid Valve
J. Beta blocker
L. Good Samaritan
N. Sympathetic Nervous System
P. Third degree Heart Block
R. Tachycardia
T. Implantable Defibrillator
V. LAD
X. Pulmonary Artery
Z. Catheter

Provide the word that best matches each clue.

131. _____ Inner surface of the heart.

132. _____ The time before the cell is fully repolarized when it can respond to a stimulus.

133. _____ The medical term for a heart attack. The blockage or occlusion of a coronary artery causing the loss of blood supply to the heart muscle.

134. _____ polymorphic ventricular tachycardia characterized by QRS complexes that change directions.

© 2017 Network4Learning, Inc.

135. _____ Tachycardia with rate > 150bpm; no P waves can be identified.

136. _____ Low pressure cardiac chamber that receives blood from the Right Atrium and pumps it into the pulmonary artery.

137. _____ A congenital heart defect where an abnormal opening in the septum separates the ventricles.

138. _____ One-way valve that allow blood flow from Right Atrium to Right Ventricle.

139. _____ An ECG complex that appears earlier than expected that originates from an ectopic focus in the ventricles.

140. _____ The upper chamber of each half of the heart.

141. _____ Rapid, fluttering heart beats. Heart palpitations can be triggered by exercise, medications, or stress.

142. _____ A series of advanced treatments for cardiac arrest and other life-threatening conditions.

143. _____ Large vein that carries deoxygenated blood from the lower venous circulation (below the neck) and empties into the Right Atrium.

144. _____ Antiarrhythmic infusion for stable wide QRS Tachycardia. Used to treat life-threatening ventricular tachycardia or symptomatic PVC's.

145. _____ A technique to remove or render inactive problematic cardiac tissue.

146. _____ High pressure chamber of the heart responsible for pumping oxygenated blood to the systemic circulation.

147. _____ An ECG complex that appears earlier than expected; originates from ectopic focus in atrium.

© 2017 Network4Learning, Inc.

148. _____ A medical procedure by which a trained professional converts an abnormally fast heart rate to a normal rate using defibrillation.

149. _____ A test that measures and records the electrical activity in the heart.

150. _____ A normal heart rate.

151. _____ A non-profit organization that establishes the standards in cardiac care.

152. _____ A medical term to describe the normal beating of the heart.

153. _____ A form of ultrasound that can detect blood flow. Used to diagnose cardiac disease.

154. _____ A rapid heart rhythm resulting in 160-190 beats per minute and is a type of supraventricular tachycardia.

155. _____ Current from a defibrillator is delivered two ways. Biphasic therapy was introduced in the 1990s and lowers the electrical threshold for successful defibrillation.

156. _____ The 1st positive deflection following the P wave.

A. Ablation
C. Premature Atrial Contraction
E. Biphasic Energy
G. ACLS
I. Palpitation
K. Sinus Rhythm
M. Right Ventricle
O. Endocardium
Q. Normal Sinus Rhythm
S. Left Ventricle
U. Cardioversion
W. Tricuspid Valve
Y. American Heart Association

B. Myocardial Infarction
D. Atrial Tachycardia
F. Electrocardiogram
H. Inferior Vena Cava
J. Procainamide
L. Ventricular Septal Defect
N. Torsades de Pointes
P. Premature Ventricular Contraction
R. Supraventricular Tachycardia
T. Doppler Ultrasound
V. Atrium
X. R wave
Z. Relative Refractory Period

© 2017 Network4Learning, Inc.

Provide the word that best matches each clue.

1. LEFT ATRIUM

    The upper left chamber of the heart that receives oxygenated blood from the lungs and pumps it to the left ventricle.

2. FIRST DEGREE BLOCK

    Normal Sinus Rhythm with PR interval > 0.20.

3. ACLS

    A series of advanced treatments for cardiac arrest and other life-threatening conditions.

4. TRABECULAE

    Smooth ridges on the walls of the heart.

5. ATRIAL TACHYCARDIA

    A rapid heart rhythm resulting in 160-190 beats per minute and is a type of supraventricular tachycardia.

6. MITRAL VALVE

    One-way valve that allow blood flow from the Left Atrium to the Left Ventricle and prevents blood from flowing back to the LA during Ventricular systole.

7. LIDOCAINE ACTION

    Anti-arrhythmic that increases electrical threshold of ventricles during diastole

8. PULMONARY VALVE

    One-way valve between low pressure Right Ventricle and low pressure Pulmonary artery. Allows blood flow from Right Ventricle to Pulmonary Artery and prevents blood from flowing back to RV during vent. diastole.

9. SYMPATHETIC NERVOUS SYSTEM

    Innervates all parts of the heart and all the blood vessels.

10. ASYSTOLE

    Absence of a heartbeat, also known as "flat line". A dire condition in which the heart has no rhythm.

11. DEFIBRILLATION

    The act of using equipment to send an electrical shock to the heart to stop an irregular heart rhythm. Defibrillation is the only cure to sudden cardiac arrest.

12. ELECTROCARDIOGRAM

    A test that measures and records the electrical activity in the heart.

© 2017 Network4Learning, Inc.

13. BETA BLOCKER	Used in stable symptomatic tachycardia that is persistent and does not have a wide QRS.
14. CONGENITAL HEART DEFECT	A birth defect of the heart
15. TORSADES DE POINTES	polymorphic ventricular tachycardia characterized by QRS complexes that change directions.
16. PREMATURE JUNCTIONAL CONTRACTION	An ECG complex that appears earlier than expected than originates from an ectopic focus in the AV junction.
17. MANUAL DEFIBRILLATOR	An advanced life support medical device that monitors the heart rhythm and allow the user to manually set the energy delivery and deliver a shock.
18. FIBRILLATION	A rapid twitching of the heart muscles caused by an abnormal and sometimes chaotic discharge of electrical impulses. Atrial fibrillation results in a rapid and irregular heartbeat.
19. RIGHT CORONARY ARTERY	Coronary artery that delivers blood to the Right Ventricle, AV junction, and the SA node in 55% of the population.
20. INFERIOR VENA CAVA	Large vein that carries deoxygenated blood from the lower venous circulation (below the neck) and empties into the Right Atrium.
21. CATHETER	A thin, flexible tube that is inserted into the heart through a peripheral blood vessel to provide therapy and
22. HEART RATE	The number of complete cycles of the contraction and relaxation of the heart muscle per minute. A normal heart rate for adults is 60 to 100 beats per minute.
23. TROPOMYOSIN	At the beginning of contraction, calcium is released and attaches to troponin, allowing cross bridges on the myosin to attach to the actin.
24. JUNCTIONAL TACHYCARDIA	Junction rhythm with a rate > 100bpm

© 2017 Network4Learning, Inc.

25. ALGORITHM _____ A set of precise rules programmed into a defibrillator to analyze heart rhythms and treat cardiac arrest.

26. SA NODE _____ Primary pacemaker of the heart. The intrinsic rate of the SA node is 60-100 bpm

A. Fibrillation
C. Heart Rate
E. Junctional Tachycardia
G. Asystole
I. Electrocardiogram
K. Torsades de Pointes
M. Sympathetic Nervous System
O. Beta blocker
Q. Lidocaine action
S. Defibrillation
U. Algorithm
W. Catheter
Y. First degree block

B. SA Node
D. Pulmonary Valve
F. Right Coronary Artery
H. Tropomyosin
J. Atrial Tachycardia
L. Inferior Vena Cava
N. ACLS
P. Premature Junctional Contraction
R. Congenital Heart Defect
T. Trabeculae
V. Left Atrium
X. Manual Defibrillator
Z. Mitral Valve

Provide the word that best matches each clue.

27. STENT _____ A tube designed to be implanted in a vessel to help keep it open.

28. LEFT ATRIUM _____ Low pressure chamber that receives oxygenated blood from the pulmonary system via the pulmonary veins.

29. ISUPREL _____ Used for heart block and ventricular arrhythmias. A sympathomimetic that results in pronounced stimulation of beta1 & beta2 receptors of heart and bronchi.

30. VASOPRESSIN _____ Alternate with epinephrine in patient with pulseless VFib

31. ASYSTOLE _____ Absence of a heartbeat, also known as "flat line". A dire condition in which the heart has no rhythm.

32. RELATIVE REFRACTORY PERIOD _____ The time before the cell is fully repolarized when it can respond to a stimulus.

33. RIGHT VENTRICLE _____ The lower right chamber of the heart that receives deoxygenated blood from the right atrium and pumps it to the lungs through the pulmonary artery.

© 2017 Network4Learning, Inc.

34. JUNCTIONAL RHYTHMS	Rhythms initiated from impulses that originate from the Atrial Ventricular junction. Intrinsic rate 40-60bpm.
35. VENTRICULAR TACHYCARDIA	Impulse for ventricular contraction originated from ventricle with a rate of > 100pbm.
36. BUNDLE OF HIS	Conducts impulses from AV node to bundle branches; makes up AV junction
37. SYMPATHETIC NERVOUS SYSTEM	Innervates all parts of the heart and all the blood vessels.
38. INFERIOR VENA CAVA	Large vein that carries deoxygenated blood from the lower venous circulation (below the neck) and empties into the Right Atrium.
39. CARDIOVERSION	A medical procedure by which a trained professional converts an abnormally fast heart rate to a normal rate using defibrillation.
40. SUDDEN CARDIAC ARREST	The sudden, unexpected loss of the heart function, resulting in the loss of effective blood flow.
41. PR INTERVAL	Measured from where the P-wave starts to where the QRS first leaves the isoelectric line. Represents atrial depolarization and the delay in the AV node.
42. EPICARDIUM	Outer surface of the heart.
43. JUNCTIONAL TACHYCARDIA	Junction rhythm with a rate > 100bpm
44. P WAVE	Part of the ECG complex that reflects atrial depolarization.
45. CARDIOPULMONARY RESUSCITATION	An emergency procedure treating a victim who is unconscious and unresponsive with no signs of circulation.
46. EPINEPHRINE	Sympathomimetic that stimulates alpha, beta 1&2 receptors resulting in cardiac stimulation.
47. Q WAVE	The first negative deflection following the P wave.
48. LEFT VENTRICLE	High pressure chamber of the heart responsible for pumping oxygenated blood to the systemic circulation.

© 2017 Network4Learning, Inc.

49. BIPHASIC ENERGY

Current from a defibrillator is delivered two ways. Biphasic therapy was introduced in the 1990s and lowers the electrical threshold for successful defibrillation.

50. VENTRICULAR TACHYCARDIA

A fast heart rhythm that originates in the ventricles. Also known as V-tach.

51. RIGHT CORONARY ARTERY

Coronary artery that delivers blood to the Right Ventricle, AV junction, and the SA node in 55% of the population.

52. SUPRAVENTRICULAR TACHYCARDIA

A rapid rhythm of the heart, with a pulse of 150-250 beats per minute. The condition can last a few minutes or even days. Treatment may come in the form of cardioversion.

A. Epicardium
B. Relative Refractory Period
C. Cardioversion
D. Sudden Cardiac Arrest
E. Vasopressin
F. Right Ventricle
G. Bundle of His
H. Inferior Vena Cava
I. Ventricular Tachycardia
J. Asystole
K. Biphasic Energy
L. PR interval
M. Epinephrine
N. Junctional Rhythms
O. Supraventricular Tachycardia
P. Isuprel
Q. Cardiopulmonary Resuscitation
R. Sympathetic Nervous System
S. Left Atrium
T. Ventricular Tachycardia
U. Right Coronary Artery
V. Q wave
W. Stent
X. Left Ventricle
Y. Junctional Tachycardia
Z. P Wave

Provide the word that best matches each clue.

53. DOPAMINE

Sympathomimetic agent that causes peripheral vasoconstriction (alpha effects) and muscle vasodilation (beta effects).

54. VENTRICULAR FIBRILLATION

The most common form of sudden cardiac arrest. A sudden, lethal arrhythmia in which chaotic electrical activity results in the ventricles fluttering rapidly and losing the ability to pump blood.

55. LEFT ATRIUM

Low pressure chamber that receives oxygenated blood from the pulmonary system via the pulmonary veins.

56. DOPPLER ULTRASOUND

A form of ultrasound that can detect blood flow. Used to diagnose cardiac disease.

© 2017 Network4Learning, Inc.

57. ABLATION — A technique to remove or render inactive problematic cardiac tissue.

58. MAGNESIUM SULFATE — Treats Torsades de Pointes, Ventricular Fibrillation. Electrolyte that causes all muscles to contract. Results in depression early after depolarization.

59. CHAIN OF SURVIVAL — A four-step process for treating victims of sudden cardiac arrest.

60. ATRIUM — The upper chamber of each half of the heart.

61. ENLARGED HEART — An unusually large heart. This condition can be a a result of conditions such as an abnormal heart rhythm, stress, or weakening of the heart muscle.

62. CARDIOPULMONARY RESUSCITATION — An emergency procedure treating a victim who is unconscious and unresponsive with no signs of circulation.

63. CPR — cardiopulmonary resuscitation.

64. ISUPREL — Used for heart block and ventricular arrhythmias. A sympathomimetic that results in pronounced stimulation of beta1 & beta2 receptors of heart and bronchi.

65. SUDDEN CARDIAC ARREST — The sudden, unexpected loss of the heart function, resulting in the loss of effective blood flow.

66. P WAVE — Part of the ECG complex that reflects atrial depolarization.

67. JOULES — A measure of electrical energy equal to the work done when a current of one ampere passes through a resistance of one ohm for one second.

68. PARASYMPATHETIC NERVOUS SYSTEM — Medulla and mediated by vagus nerve; slows Heart Rate, decreases speed of conduction through AV node, slight depression in contractility.

69. CARDIAC TAMPONADE — Constriction of the heart that prevent filling of the ventricles. It is usually caused by fluid or blood accumulating in the pericardial sac.

© 2017 Network4Learning, Inc.

70. VASOPRESSIN — Alternate with epinephrine in patient with pulseless VFib

71. PR INTERVAL — Measured from where the P-wave starts to where the QRS first leaves the isoelectric line. Represents atrial depolarization and the delay in the AV node.

72. DEFIBRILLATION — The act of using equipment to send an electrical shock to the heart to stop an irregular heart rhythm. Defibrillation is the only cure to sudden cardiac arrest.

73. STROKE VOLUME — Amount of blood ejected with each ventricular contraction.

74. RELATIVE REFRACTORY PERIOD — The time before the cell is fully repolarized when it can respond to a stimulus.

75. CARDIAC OUTPUT — The amount of blood ejected by the heart in one minute in liters

76. BETA BLOCKER — Used in stable symptomatic tachycardia that is persistent and does not have a wide QRS.

77. VASOVAGAL RESPONSE — Caused by stimulation of para-sympathetic Nervous System and results in slowing of the Heart Rate. Can be initiated intentionally with carotid massage or valsalva maneuver.

78. LAD — Coronary artery that supplies oxygenated blood to the anterior surface of the left ventricle, the ventricular septum, and the papillary muscles of the mitral valve and the bundle of His.

A. Stroke Volume
B. Left Atrium
C. Ventricular Fibrillation
D. Vasovagal Response
E. Magnesium sulfate
F. Cardiac Tamponade
G. Sudden Cardiac Arrest
H. P Wave
I. Chain of Survival
J. Cardiopulmonary Resuscitation
K. Ablation
L. Doppler Ultrasound
M. PR interval
N. Relative Refractory Period
O. Cardiac Output
P. Dopamine
Q. Parasympathetic Nervous System
R. CPR
S. Vasopressin
T. Joules
U. Isuprel
V. LAD
W. Enlarged Heart
X. Defibrillation
Y. Beta blocker
Z. Atrium

© 2017 Network4Learning, Inc.

Provide the word that best matches each clue.

79. VENTRICULAR BIGEMINY — PVC that occurs with every other beat.

80. PAROXYSMAL ATRIAL TACHYCARDIA — Atrial tachycardia that starts and stops suddenly.

81. AMIODARONE — Anti-arrhythmic used to treat atrial-ventricular tachyarrhythmias.

82. AED — A life-saving device that treats sudden cardiac arrest.

83. MYOCARDIAL INFARCTION — The medical term for a heart attack. The blockage or occlusion of a coronary artery causing the loss of blood supply to the heart muscle.

84. IDIOVENTRICULAR RHYTHM — Originates in the ventricle. Rate is 20-40bpm.

85. JUNCTIONAL RHYTHMS — Rhythms initiated from impulses that originate from the Atrial Ventricular junction. Intrinsic rate 40-60bpm.

86. REPOLARIZATION — Return of membrane potential to its resting state. K+ move into the cell and Na+ moves out.

87. PREMATURE JUNCTIONAL CONTRACTION — An ECG complex that appears earlier than expected than originates from an ectopic focus in the AV junction.

88. ATRIAL FIBRILLATION — An abnormal, very fast and disorganized heart rate with chaotic electrical activity in the atria of the heart.

89. ARRHYTHMIA — An abnormality or irregularity in the heart rhythm.

90. JOULES — A measure of electrical energy equal to the work done when a current of one ampere passes through a resistance of one ohm for one second.

91. VALSALVA MANEUVER — A forceful attempt at expiration when the airway is closed to stop supraventricular tachycardia.

92. VASOPRESSIN — Alternate with epinephrine in patient with pulseless VFib

© 2017 Network4Learning, Inc.

93. ATRIAL TACHYCARDIA

A rapid heart rhythm resulting in 160-190 beats per minute and is a type of supraventricular tachycardia.

94. MOBITZ II

A heart block where some P waves not conducted through AV node. Some P waves not followed by QRS complexes. P waves that do follow QRS, have consistent intervals.

95. LIDOCAINE ACTION

Anti-arrhythmic that increases electrical threshold of ventricles during diastole

96. TRABECULAE

Smooth ridges on the walls of the heart.

97. BUNDLE OF HIS

Conducts impulses from AV node to bundle branches; makes up AV junction

98. ATROPINE

Para-sympatholytic that blocks acetylcholine effects on post cholinergic receptors in smooth muscle and SA-AV nodes.

99. SINUS ARREST

A pause caused by the SA node not firing; pause measures more than 2 R-R intervals.

100. TROPOMYOSIN

At the beginning of contraction, calcium is released and attaches to troponin, allowing cross bridges on the myosin to attach to the actin.

101. TACHYCARDIA

A rapid heart rate, usually over 100 beats per minute.

102. ACLS

A series of advanced treatments for cardiac arrest and other life-threatening conditions.

103. LEFT VENTRICLE

The lower left chamber of the heart that receives oxygenated blood from the left atrium and pumps the blood through the aorta to the body.

104. LEFT VENTRICULAR DYSFUNCTION

A condition in which the left ventricle of the heart exhibits decreased functionality. This can lead to heart failure.

A. Vasopressin
C. Trabeculae
E. Mobitz II

B. Left Ventricular Dysfunction
D. Sinus Arrest
F. Premature Junctional Contraction

© 2017 Network4Learning, Inc.

G. Repolarization
I. Paroxysmal Atrial Tachycardia
K. Valsalva Maneuver
M. Joules
O. ACLS
Q. Atrial Tachycardia
S. Bundle of His
U. Tachycardia
W. Left Ventricle
Y. Atropine

H. AED
J. Myocardial Infarction
L. Lidocaine action
N. Ventricular Bigeminy
P. Junctional Rhythms
R. Idioventricular Rhythm
T. Tropomyosin
V. Arrhythmia
X. Amiodarone
Z. Atrial Fibrillation

Provide the word that best matches each clue.

105. VENTRICULAR BIGEMINY — PVC that occurs with every other beat.

106. VENTRICULAR TACHYCARDIA — Impulse for ventricular contraction originated from ventricle with a rate of > 100pbm.

107. ACLS — A series of advanced treatments for cardiac arrest and other life-threatening conditions.

108. AMIODARONE — Anti-arrhythmic used to treat atrial-ventricular tachyarrhythmias.

109. PREMATURE VENTRICULAR CONTRACTION — An ECG complex that appears earlier than expected that originates from an ectopic focus in the ventricles.

110. SYMPATHETIC NERVOUS SYSTEM — Innervates all parts of the heart and all the blood vessels.

111. GOOD SAMARITAN — Immunity protection provided by each state government and the Federal government to encourage lay responders to treat a victim of sudden cardiac arrest with an AED and CPR.

112. PROCAINAMIDE — Antiarrhythmic infusion for stable wide QRS Tachycardia. Used to treat life-threatening ventricular tachycardia or symptomatic PVC's.

113. AED — A life-saving device that treats sudden cardiac arrest.

© 2017 Network4Learning, Inc.

114. LAD _____ Coronary artery that supplies oxygenated blood to the anterior surface of the left ventricle, the ventricular septum, and the papillary muscles of the mitral valve and the bundle of His.

115. CATHETER _____ A thin, flexible tube that is inserted into the heart through a peripheral blood vessel to provide therapy and

116. THIRD DEGREE HEART BLOCK _____ Independent activity of atria and ventricles

117. SUDDEN CARDIAC DEATH _____ Death as a result of sudden cardiac arrest.

118. INTRINSIC RATE _____ The normal rate for a given pacemaker cells.

119. SINUS EXIT BLOCK _____ Pause when impulse not conducted out of SA node; pause is exactly 2 R-R intervals.

120. PULMONARY ARTERY _____ Vessel that delivers blood from the Left Ventricle to Pulmonary veins.

121. TACHYCARDIA _____ A rapid heart rate, usually over 100 beats per minute.

122. MOBITZ I _____ A heart block where the PR interval becomes progressively longer until the P wave is not conducted through the ventricle and a QRS complex is dropped.

123. SINUS RHYTHM _____ A medical term to describe the normal beating of the heart.

124. TRICUSPID VALVE _____ One-way valve that allow blood flow from Right Atrium to Right Ventricle.

125. BETA BLOCKER _____ Used in stable symptomatic tachycardia that is persistent and does not have a wide QRS.

126. VASOPRESSIN _____ Alternate with epinephrine in patient with pulseless VFib

© 2017 Network4Learning, Inc.

127. CARDIAC TAMPONADE _____ Constriction of the heart that prevent filling of the ventricles. It is usually caused by fluid or blood accumulating in the pericardial sac.

128. INOTROPIC EFFECT _____ Increases force of muscle contraction.

129. CALCIUM CHANNEL BLOCKER _____ Used in stable symptomatic tachycardias that are persistent and do not have wide QRS-Treatment for Afib., and PSVT.

130. IMPLANTABLE DEFIBRILLATOR _____ A medical device that is implanted in the body to diagnose and treat abnormal electrical arrhythmias. If an abnormal arrhythmia is detected, the ICD will apply a shock to restore the heart to a normal rhythm.

A. Amiodarone
C. ACLS
E. Ventricular Bigeminy
G. Calcium channel blocker
I. Cardiac Tamponade
K. Sinus Exit Block
M. Vasopressin
O. Mobitz I
Q. Sudden Cardiac Death
S. Intrinsic Rate
U. AED
W. Procainamide
Y. Inotropic Effect

B. Premature Ventricular Contraction
D. Ventricular Tachycardia
F. Sinus Rhythm
H. Tricuspid Valve
J. Beta blocker
L. Good Samaritan
N. Sympathetic Nervous System
P. Third degree Heart Block
R. Tachycardia
T. Implantable Defibrillator
V. LAD
X. Pulmonary Artery
Z. Catheter

Provide the word that best matches each clue.

131. ENDOCARDIUM _____ Inner surface of the heart.

132. RELATIVE REFRACTORY PERIOD ____ The time before the cell is fully repolarized when it can respond to a stimulus.

133. MYOCARDIAL INFARCTION _____ The medical term for a heart attack. The blockage or occlusion of a coronary artery causing the loss of blood supply to the heart muscle.

134. TORSADES DE POINTES _____ polymorphic ventricular tachycardia characterized by QRS complexes that change directions.

© 2017 Network4Learning, Inc.

135. SUPRAVENTRICULAR TACHYCARDIA — Tachycardia with rate > 150bpm; no P waves can be identified.

136. RIGHT VENTRICLE — Low pressure cardiac chamber that receives blood from the Right Atrium and pumps it into the pulmonary artery.

137. VENTRICULAR SEPTAL DEFECT — A congenital heart defect where an abnormal opening in the septum separates the ventricles.

138. TRICUSPID VALVE — One-way valve that allow blood flow from Right Atrium to Right Ventricle.

139. PREMATURE VENTRICULAR CONTRACTION — An ECG complex that appears earlier than expected that originates from an ectopic focus in the ventricles.

140. ATRIUM — The upper chamber of each half of the heart.

141. PALPITATION — Rapid, fluttering heart beats. Heart palpitations can be triggered by exercise, medications, or stress.

142. ACLS — A series of advanced treatments for cardiac arrest and other life-threatening conditions.

143. INFERIOR VENA CAVA — Large vein that carries deoxygenated blood from the lower venous circulation (below the neck) and empties into the Right Atrium.

144. PROCAINAMIDE — Antiarrhythmic infusion for stable wide QRS Tachycardia. Used to treat life-threatening ventricular tachycardia or symptomatic PVC's.

145. ABLATION — A technique to remove or render inactive problematic cardiac tissue.

146. LEFT VENTRICLE — High pressure chamber of the heart responsible for pumping oxygenated blood to the systemic circulation.

147. PREMATURE ATRIAL CONTRACTION — An ECG complex that appears earlier than expected; originates from ectopic focus in atrium.

© 2017 Network4Learning, Inc.

148. CARDIOVERSION _____   A medical procedure by which a trained professional converts an abnormally fast heart rate to a normal rate using defibrillation.

149. ELECTROCARDIOGRAM _____   A test that measures and records the electrical activity in the heart.

150. NORMAL SINUS RHYTHM _____   A normal heart rate.

151. AMERICAN HEART ASSOCIATION _____   A non-profit organization that establishes the standards in cardiac care.

152. SINUS RHYTHM _____   A medical term to describe the normal beating of the heart.

153. DOPPLER ULTRASOUND _____   A form of ultrasound that can detect blood flow. Used to diagnose cardiac disease.

154. ATRIAL TACHYCARDIA _____   A rapid heart rhythm resulting in 160-190 beats per minute and is a type of supraventricular tachycardia.

155. BIPHASIC ENERGY _____   Current from a defibrillator is delivered two ways. Biphasic therapy was introduced in the 1990s and lowers the electrical threshold for successful defibrillation.

156. R WAVE _____   The 1st positive deflection following the P wave.

A. Ablation
B. Myocardial Infarction
C. Premature Atrial Contraction
D. Atrial Tachycardia
E. Biphasic Energy
F. Electrocardiogram
G. ACLS
H. Inferior Vena Cava
I. Palpitation
J. Procainamide
K. Sinus Rhythm
L. Ventricular Septal Defect
M. Right Ventricle
N. Torsades de Pointes
O. Endocardium
P. Premature Ventricular Contraction
Q. Normal Sinus Rhythm
R. Supraventricular Tachycardia
S. Left Ventricle
T. Doppler Ultrasound
U. Cardioversion
V. Atrium
W. Tricuspid Valve
X. R wave
Y. American Heart Association
Z. Relative Refractory Period

© 2017 Network4Learning, Inc.

Word Search

1. *Find the hidden words. The words have been placed horizontally, vertically, or diagonally. When you locate a word, draw a circle around it.*

I	D	A	T	R	I	A	L	T	A	C	H	Y	C	A	R	D	I	A	J
M	A	N	U	A	L	D	E	F	I	B	R	I	L	L	A	T	O	R	O
O	W	Y	G	C	N	P	A	C	E	M	A	K	E	R	X	U	C	P	U
E	K	P	R	I	G	H	T	V	E	N	T	R	I	C	L	E	K	U	L
P	R	O	C	A	I	N	A	M	I	D	E	V	D	I	P	F	M	S	E
G	A	T	R	I	A	L	F	I	B	R	I	L	L	A	T	I	O	N	S
K	F	R	I	G	H	T	A	T	R	I	U	M	T	P	J	X	B	W	B
O	C	R	E	A	R	R	H	Y	T	H	M	I	A	G	Q	H	I	Y	G
O	I	V	T	N	E	P	I	N	E	P	H	R	I	N	E	L	T	I	Z
B	I	P	H	A	S	I	C	E	N	E	R	G	Y	W	W	H	Z	X	B
V	A	L	S	A	L	V	A	M	A	N	E	U	V	E	R	H	I	C	K
I	L	T	N	M	E	Z	C	A	T	H	E	T	E	R	X	B	I	A	C

1. Current from a defibrillator is delivered two ways. Biphasic therapy was introduced in the 1990s and lowers the electrical threshold for successful defibrillation.
2. An abnormality or irregularity in the heart rhythm.
3. The lower right chamber of the heart that receives deoxygenated blood from the right atrium and pumps it to the lungs through the pulmonary artery.
4. A rapid heart rhythm resulting in 160-190 beats per minute and is a type of supraventricular tachycardia.
5. A measure of electrical energy equal to the work done when a current of one ampere passes through a resistance of one ohm for one second.
6. An implantable medical device that sends electrical signals to the heart to set the heart rhythm.
7. An advanced life support medical device that monitors the heart rhythm and allow the user to manually set the energy delivery and deliver a shock.
8. A heart block where some P waves not conducted through AV node. Some P waves not followed by QRS complexes. P waves that do follow QRS, have consistent intervals.
9. A thin, flexible tube that is inserted into the heart through a peripheral blood vessel to provide therapy and
10. Antiarrhythmic infusion for stable wide QRS Tachycardia. Used to treat life-threatening ventricular tachycardia or symptomatic PVC's.
11. An abnormal, very fast and disorganized heart rate with chaotic electrical activity in the atria of the heart.
12. A forceful attempt at expiration when the airway is closed to stop supraventricular tachycardia.
13. Sympathomimetic that stimulates alpha, beta 1&2 receptors resulting in cardiac stimulation.
14. Low pressure cardiac chamber that receives deoxygenated blood from the systemic venous circulation via the inferior vena cava and the superior vena cava.

A. Joules
E. Atrial Fibrillation
I. Biphasic Energy
M. Procainamide
B. Valsalva Maneuver
F. Mobitz II
J. Epinephrine
N. Catheter
C. Manual Defibrillator
G. Right Ventricle
K. Atrial Tachycardia
D. Right Atrium
H. Pacemaker
L. Arrhythmia

© 2017 Network4Learning, Inc.

2. *Find the hidden words. The words have been placed horizontally, vertically, or diagonally. When you locate a word, draw a circle around it.*

R	I	G	H	T	C	O	R	O	N	A	R	Y	A	R	T	E	R	Y	T
L	D	A	C	L	S	E	O	E	C	A	R	O	N	T	P	V	C	X	X
N	W	T	C	A	R	D	I	O	V	E	R	S	I	O	N	K	Q	N	A
P	D	H	E	A	R	T	M	U	R	M	U	R	N	U	O	T	Y	E	M
O	L	T	K	I	T	R	I	C	U	S	P	I	D	V	A	L	V	E	O
Y	S	N	J	P	P	U	R	K	I	N	J	E	F	I	B	E	R	S	B
C	A	R	D	I	A	C	T	A	M	P	O	N	A	D	E	O	S	S	I
T	S	Y	C	O	R	O	N	A	R	Y	S	I	N	U	S	H	F	N	T
U	O	Z	C	W	R	H	E	A	R	T	R	A	T	E	Y	I	X	M	Z
H	F	R	F	Z	Z	L	E	F	T	V	E	N	T	R	I	C	L	E	I
T	J	P	O	Z	Q	W	A	V	E	V	J	K	F	L	U	T	T	E	R
U	B	E	L	E	C	T	R	O	C	A	R	D	I	O	G	R	A	M	U

1. Venous drainage system of the heart. Returns de-oxygenated blood from the heart to the Right Atrium.
2. The first negative deflection following the P wave.
3. The lower left chamber of the heart that receives oxygenated blood from the left atrium and pumps the blood through the aorta to the body.
4. Coronary artery that delivers blood to the Right Ventricle, AV junction, and the SA node in 55% of the population.
5. A PVC that falls on or very near the T wave.
6. An abnormal "whooshing" sound made by blood flowing through the heart.
7. A test that measures and records the electrical activity in the heart.
8. One-way valve that allow blood flow from Right Atrium to Right Ventricle.
9. A rapid, but organized vibration of the heart muscle. Atrial flutter can result in 250-350 heart beats per minute.
10. A heart block where the PR interval becomes progressively longer until the P wave is not conducted through the ventricle and a QRS complex is dropped.
11. A medical procedure by which a trained professional converts an abnormally fast heart rate to a normal rate using defibrillation.
12. Constriction of the heart that prevent filling of the ventricles. It is usually caused by fluid or blood accumulating in the pericardial sac.
13. The number of complete cycles of the contraction and relaxation of the heart muscle per minute. A normal heart rate for adults is 60 to 100 beats per minute.
14. Final part of the conduction system that initiates vent. depolarization.
15. Continuous monitoring of the electrical activity of a patient's heart with a small, portable ECG machine. The device is typically worn around the neck or waist for a 24-hour period.
16. Low pressure cardiac chamber that receives blood from the Right Atrium and pumps it into the pulmonary artery.
17. A series of advanced treatments for cardiac arrest and other life-threatening conditions.
18. Para-sympatholytic that blocks acetylcholine effects on post cholinergic receptors in smooth muscle and SA-AV nodes.
19. The act of using equipment to send an electrical shock to the heart to stop an irregular heart rhythm. Defibrillation is the only cure to sudden cardiac arrest.

A. Right Coronary Artery
E. Cardiac Tamponade
I. Purkinje Fibers
M. Defibrillation
Q. Heart Murmur

B. Tricuspid Valve
F. Coronary Sinus
J. Electrocardiogram
N. Atropine
R. Left Ventricle

C. R ON T PVC
G. Right Ventricle
K. Mobitz I
O. Cardioversion
S. Holter Monitoring

D. Flutter
H. Q wave
L. Heart Rate
P. ACLS

© 2017 Network4Learning, Inc.

3. Find the hidden words. The words have been placed horizontally, vertically, or diagonally. When you locate a word, draw a circle around it.

H	V	K	O	N	I	C	A	R	D	I	O	V	E	R	S	I	O	N	F
D	P	O	M	A	G	N	E	S	I	U	M	S	U	L	F	A	T	E	I
W	C	O	M	M	O	T	I	O	C	O	R	D	I	S	T	J	P	U	A
B	K	W	N	S	T	G	O	O	D	S	A	M	A	R	I	T	A	N	Z
P	R	L	I	D	O	C	A	I	N	E	A	C	T	I	O	N	Q	O	Z
S	I	N	U	S	E	X	I	T	B	L	O	C	K	F	P	H	V	W	Q
S	T	R	O	K	E	V	O	L	U	M	E	M	N	X	T	W	M	C	K
K	K	M	T	R	I	C	U	S	P	I	D	V	A	L	V	E	W	E	J
R	I	G	H	T	C	O	R	O	N	A	R	Y	A	R	T	E	R	Y	A
I	I	K	E	H	S	I	N	U	S	A	R	R	E	S	T	P	B	L	Z
W	R	R	V	A	S	O	V	A	G	A	L	R	E	S	P	O	N	S	E
D	J	Z	B	B	W	S	J	O	U	L	E	S	D	H	D	H	O	K	K

1. A measure of electrical energy equal to the work done when a current of one ampere passes through a resistance of one ohm for one second.
2. A disruption of the heart rhythm caused by a sudden blunt blow to the chest.
3. Anti-arrhythmic that increases electrical threshold of ventricles during diastole
4. Immunity protection provided by each state government and the Federal government to encourage lay responders to treat a victim of sudden cardiac arrest with an AED and CPR.
5. Pause when impulse not conducted out of SA node; pause is exactly 2 R-R intervals.
6. A pause caused by the SA node not firing; pause measures more than 2 R-R intervals.
7. One-way valve that allow blood flow from Right Atrium to Right Ventricle.
8. Caused by stimulation of para-sympathetic Nervous System and results in slowing of the Heart Rate. Can be initiated intentionally with carotid massage or valsalva maneuver.
9. Amount of blood ejected with each ventricular contraction.
10. A medical procedure by which a trained professional converts an abnormally fast heart rate to a normal rate using defibrillation.
11. Coronary artery that delivers blood to the Right Ventricle, AV junction, and the SA node in 55% of the population.
12. Treats Torsades de Pointes, Ventricular Fibrillation. Electrolyte that causes all muscles to contract. Results in depression early after depolarization.
13. The sudden, unexpected loss of the heart function, resulting in the loss of effective blood flow.
14. The act of using equipment to send an electrical shock to the heart to stop an irregular heart rhythm. Defibrillation is the only cure to sudden cardiac arrest.
15. polymorphic ventricular tachycardia characterized by QRS complexes that change directions.

A. Magnesium sulfate
B. Torsades de Pointes
C. Stroke Volume
D. Joules
E. Sudden Cardiac Arrest
F. Sinus Exit Block
G. Vasovagal Response
H. Tricuspid Valve
I. Right Coronary Artery
J. Commotio Cordis
K. Cardioversion
L. Lidocaine action
M. Sinus Arrest
N. Good Samaritan
O. Defibrillation

© 2017 Network4Learning, Inc.

4. *Find the hidden words. The words have been placed horizontally, vertically, or diagonally. When you locate a word, draw a circle around it.*

I	J		C	H	A	I	N		O	F		S	U	R	V	I	V	A	L
P	D	V	B	I	P	H	A	S	I	C	E	N	E	R	G	Y	M	E	Y
X	G	X	Q	P	A	P	B	K	B	Y	X	E	U	Y	A	K	I	K	Z
L	G	T	F	W	D	L	O	N	G	Q	T	S	Y	N	D	R	O	M	E
A	W	T	W	A	E	G	S	V	P	R	I	N	T	E	R	V	A	L	V
B	F	M	E	V	N	M	T	E	L	H	R	S	F	E	Q	W	A	V	E
K	J	Q	M	E	O	S	I	N	U	S	E	X	I	T	B	L	O	C	K
H	Y	G	T	W	S	A	Y	S	I	N	U	S	A	R	R	E	S	T	F
R	I	N	T	R	I	N	S	I	C	R	A	T	E	J	O	U	L	E	S
F	A	W	T	V	N	S	E	P	I	C	A	R	D	I	U	M	G	C	W
Y	I	T	N	R	E	E	Y	H	E	A	R	T	M	U	R	M	U	R	R
V	A	S	O	V	A	G	A	L	R	E	S	P	O	N	S	E	U	O	O

1. An abnormal "whooshing" sound made by blood flowing through the heart.
2. Current from a defibrillator is delivered two ways. Biphasic therapy was introduced in the 1990s and lowers the electrical threshold for successful defibrillation.
3. Used to treat unstable tachy-arrhythmias if regular and monomorphic; Slows atrial conduction through AV node.
4. Caused by stimulation of para-sympathetic Nervous System and results in slowing of the Heart Rate. Can be initiated intentionally with carotid massage or valsalva maneuver.
5. A pause caused by the SA node not firing; pause measures more than 2 R-R intervals.
6. The normal rate for a given pacemaker cells.
7. Measured from where the P-wave starts to where the QRS first leaves the isoelectric line. Represents atrial depolarization and the delay in the AV node.
8. Outer surface of the heart.
9. The first negative deflection following the P wave.
10. An inherited defect of the rhythm of the heart. The QT segment of the heart beat is slightly longer than normal, so the heart takes longer to recharge itself between beats.
11. A measure of electrical energy equal to the work done when a current of one ampere passes through a resistance of one ohm for one second.
12. A four-step process for treating victims of sudden cardiac arrest.
13. Part of the ECG complex that reflects atrial depolarization.
14. Pause when impulse not conducted out of SA node; pause is exactly 2 R-R intervals.
15. Treats Torsades de Pointes, Ventricular Fibrillation. Electrolyte that causes all muscles to contract. Results in depression early after depolarization.
16. An advanced life support medical device that monitors the heart rhythm and allow the user to manually set the energy delivery and deliver a shock.

A. Sinus Arrest
E. PR interval
I. Long QT Syndrome
M. P Wave
B. Epicardium
F. Adenosine
J. Intrinsic Rate
N. Heart Murmur
C. Sinus Exit Block
G. Vasovagal Response
K. Q wave
O. Magnesium sulfate
D. Chain of Survival
H. Biphasic Energy
L. Manual Defibrillator
P. Joules

© 2017 Network4Learning, Inc.

5. *Find the hidden words. The words have been placed horizontally, vertically, or diagonally. When you locate a word, draw a circle around it.*

	C	H	A	I	N		O	F		S	U	R	V	I	V	A	L	A	Q
A	R	R	H	Y	T	H	M	I	A	M	P	A	C	E	M	A	K	E	R
D	J	Y	U	P	C	F	F	F	L	U	T	T	E	R	O	Z	U	N	D
C	P	R	Q	W	A	V	E	P	R	I	N	T	E	R	V	A	L	P	N
W	P	E	R	I	C	A	R	D	I	A	L	E	F	F	U	S	I	O	N
Z	Z	B	O	K	H	S	A	T	R	I	A	L	F	L	U	T	T	E	R
U	G	C	V	C	A	R	D	I	O	V	E	R	S	I	O	N	E	G	J
J	U	N	C	T	I	O	N	A	L	E	S	C	A	P	E	B	E	A	T
R	R	S	I	N	U	S	P	A	U	S	E	P	O	S	J	W	X	Q	A
Q	T	U	U	S	D	L	E	F	T	V	E	N	T	R	I	C	L	E	B
J	D	Y	O	P	Y	B	B	T	R	A	B	E	C	U	L	A	E	W	Q
E	N	N	H	A	Z	E	P	R	O	C	A	I	N	A	M	I	D	E	I

1. Measured from where the P-wave starts to where the QRS first leaves the isoelectric line. Represents atrial depolarization and the delay in the AV node.
2. A four-step process for treating victims of sudden cardiac arrest.
3. cardiopulmonary resuscitation.
4. A rapid, but organized vibration of the heart muscle. Atrial flutter can result in 250-350 heart beats per minute.
5. Rapid, organized atrial contractions that usually result in a heart rate of 250-350 beats per minute. AF is a form of supraventricular tachycardia.
6. Smooth ridges on the walls of the heart.
7. Complex or rhythm that takes over if SA node fails. Beats or rhythm occur after a pause and later than expected.
8. A medical procedure by which a trained professional converts an abnormally fast heart rate to a normal rate using defibrillation.
9. The first negative deflection following the P wave.
10. The lower left chamber of the heart that receives oxygenated blood from the left atrium and pumps the blood through the aorta to the body.
11. An accumulation of fluid in the pericardial sac.
12. An abnormality or irregularity in the heart rhythm.
13. Pause caused by delay in impulse being initiated in the SA node. pause is < 2 R-R intervals.
14. Antiarrhythmic infusion for stable wide QRS Tachycardia. Used to treat life-threatening ventricular tachycardia or symptomatic PVC's.
15. An implantable medical device that sends electrical signals to the heart to set the heart rhythm.
16. Death as a result of sudden cardiac arrest.

A. Sinus Pause
E. Left Ventricle
I. Chain of Survival
M. Flutter
B. Q wave
F. Arrhythmia
J. Procainamide
N. Sudden Cardiac Death
C. Pericardial Effusion
G. PR interval
K. Trabeculae
O. CPR
D. Atrial Flutter
H. Cardioversion
L. Junctional Escape Beat
P. Pacemaker

© 2017 Network4Learning, Inc.

6. *Find the hidden words. The words have been placed horizontally, vertically, or diagonally. When you locate a word, draw a circle around it.*

A	T	R	I	A	L	F	I	B	R	I	L	L	A	T	I	O	N	D	Y
O	W	E	Z	B	I	B	X	R	V	T	R	A	B	E	C	U	L	A	E
N	Y	A	T	R	I	A	L	T	A	C	H	Y	C	A	R	D	I	A	B
C	A	T	O	R	S	A	D	E	S	D	E	P	O	I	N	T	E	S	L
A	H	C	O	M	M	O	T	I	O	C	O	R	D	I	S	V	B	S	O
N	W	S	R	J	D	R	T	Q	P	U	P	L	P	T	F	M	M	Z	Y
M	G	X	D	K	I	O	R	D	R	L	M	V	Z	W	R	J	G	L	K
B	A	L	I	S	E	N	H	H	E	W	X	N	M	A	W	O	Z	B	I
I	V	U	K	C	O	T	A	O	S	Y	R	Y	Q	V	D	G	F	D	V
K	M	N	Q	U	B	P	Q	W	S	N	K	E	R	E	O	X	V	Y	I
A	L	R	Z	Z	M	V	K	U	I	A	R	R	H	Y	T	H	M	I	A
T	N	J	Q	T	R	C	I	I	N	P	R	I	N	T	E	R	V	A	L

1. A disruption of the heart rhythm caused by a sudden blunt blow to the chest.
2. A PVC that falls on or very near the T wave.
3. An abnormal, very fast and disorganized heart rate with chaotic electrical activity in the atria of the heart.
4. Ventricular repolarization; follows the QRS complex.
5. Alternate with epinephrine in patient with pulseless VFib
6. A rapid heart rhythm resulting in 160-190 beats per minute and is a type of supraventricular tachycardia.
7. An abnormality or irregularity in the heart rhythm.
8. polymorphic ventricular tachycardia characterized by QRS complexes that change directions.
9. Rhythms initiated from impulses that originate from the Atrial Ventricular junction. Intrinsic rate 40-60bpm.
10. The amount of blood ejected by the heart in one minute in liters
11. Measured from where the P-wave starts to where the QRS first leaves the isoelectric line. Represents atrial depolarization and the delay in the AV node.
12. Smooth ridges on the walls of the heart.
13. Coronary artery that delivers oxygenated blood to the left side of the heart. Divides into the left anterior descending artery and the circumflex artery.
14. The study of the electrical activity in the heart. Studies and procedures are conducted in the EP Lab of a hospital.

A. Cardiac Output
B. Torsades de Pointes
C. Left Coronary Artery
D. Commotio Cordis
E. R ON T PVC
F. Electrophysiology
G. Vasopressin
H. Junctional Rhythms
I. PR interval
J. Arrhythmia
K. Trabeculae
L. T wave
M. Atrial Fibrillation
N. Atrial Tachycardia

© 2017 Network4Learning, Inc.

7. *Find the hidden words. The words have been placed horizontally, vertically, or diagonally. When you locate a word, draw a circle around it.*

B	E	N	N	S	N	T	E	N	P	D	W	W	J	T	D	R	U	F	U
M	V	L	E	N	D	O	C	A	R	D	I	U	M	A	C	W	B	O	G
F	T	L	I	D	O	C	A	I	N	E	A	C	T	I	O	N	T	W	I
A	M	I	O	D	A	R	O	N	E	N	S	I	L	Q	N	R	M	M	J
A	T	R	I	A	L	T	A	C	H	Y	C	A	R	D	I	A	I	O	X
J	A	B	L	A	T	I	O	N	T	G	T	R	I	G	E	M	I	N	Y
L	E	F	T	V	E	N	T	R	I	C	L	E	Z	Z	L	N	W	F	T
N	K	V	M	P	U	R	K	I	N	J	E	F	I	B	E	R	S	F	X
I	M	U	L	T	I	F	O	C	A	L	P	V	C	V	J	Z	N	W	B
U	A	E	D	G	E	S	C	Z	J	B	R	O	Y	R	U	A	G	U	I
I	M	V	A	S	O	V	A	G	A	L	R	E	S	P	O	N	S	E	I
Z	V	S	T	E	N	T	A	U	A	L	P	D	N	Y	P	K	N	S	L

1. Final part of the conduction system that initiates vent. depolarization.
2. Anti-arrhythmic used to treat atrial-ventricular tachyarrhythmias.
3. Anti-arrhythmic that increases electrical threshold of ventricles during diastole
4. Inner surface of the heart.
5. Premature Ventricular contractions that originate from more than one focus.
6. The lower left chamber of the heart that receives oxygenated blood from the left atrium and pumps the blood through the aorta to the body.
7. Caused by stimulation of para-sympathetic Nervous System and results in slowing of the Heart Rate. Can be initiated intentionally with carotid massage or valsalva maneuver.
8. A tube designed to be implanted in a vessel to help keep it open.
9. A life-saving device that treats sudden cardiac arrest.
10. A technique to remove or render inactive problematic cardiac tissue.
11. Premature ventricular contractions occurring every third beat.
12. A rapid heart rhythm resulting in 160-190 beats per minute and is a type of supraventricular tachycardia.

A. Stent
E. Trigeminy
I. Lidocaine action

B. Multifocal PVC
F. Amiodarone
J. Left Ventricle

C. Endocardium
G. AED
K. Ablation

D. Atrial Tachycardia
H. Purkinje Fibers
L. Vasovagal Response

© 2017 Network4Learning, Inc.

8. *Find the hidden words. The words have been placed horizontally, vertically, or diagonally. When you locate a word, draw a circle around it.*

Q	R	S	D	U	R	A	T	I	O	N	D	O	P	A	M	I	N	E	S
V	A	T	R	I	A	L	T	A	C	H	Y	C	A	R	D	I	A	S	L
W	R	I	G	H	T	C	O	R	O	N	A	R	Y	A	R	T	E	R	Y
D	E	F	I	B	R	I	L	L	A	T	O	R	V	R	V	J	W	W	V
L	W	B	A	B	Q	A	N	B	P	Z	G	J	R	R	K	O	G	N	S
R	O	N	T	P	V	C	Y	O	W	D	C	P	N	Z	P	U	X	P	N
I	Z	D	X	F	M	Y	O	C	A	R	D	I	U	M	A	L	S	B	N
X	Y	J	Z	R	L	M	L	A	V	T	M	O	D	C	Y	E	H	R	J
G	O	B	S	A	N	O	D	E	E	L	S	L	A	T	A	S	C	L	M
R	R	E	D	O	P	P	L	E	R	U	L	T	R	A	S	O	U	N	D
V	E	N	T	R	I	C	U	L	A	R	B	I	G	E	M	I	N	Y	A
V	Z	F	D	L	R	I	G	H	T	V	E	N	T	R	I	C	L	E	E

1. A measure of electrical energy equal to the work done when a current of one ampere passes through a resistance of one ohm for one second.
2. A form of ultrasound that can detect blood flow. Used to diagnose cardiac disease.
3. Primary pacemaker of the heart. The intrinsic rate of the SA node is 60-100 bpm
4. The amount of time it takes for ventricle depolarization. Measured from when the QRS first leaves the isoelectric line to where the ST segment begins.
5. Coronary artery that delivers blood to the Right Ventricle, AV junction, and the SA node in 55% of the population.
6. The lower right chamber of the heart that receives deoxygenated blood from the right atrium and pumps it to the lungs through the pulmonary artery.
7. PVC that occurs with every other beat.
8. A rapid heart rhythm resulting in 160-190 beats per minute and is a type of supraventricular tachycardia.
9. A medical device used to treat a victim with a life-threatening irregular heart rhythm.
10. Sympathomimetic agent that causes peripheral vasoconstriction (alpha effects) and muscle vasodilation (beta effects).
11. Part of the ECG complex that reflects atrial depolarization.
12. Muscle layer of the heart.
13. A PVC that falls on or very near the T wave.
14. A kind of drug that can break up or dissolve clots blocking the flow of blood to the heart muscle. Ideally, the drug should be administered within 90 minutes of being admitted for a heart attack.
15. The medical term for a heart attack. The blockage or occlusion of a coronary artery causing the loss of blood supply to the heart muscle.
16. polymorphic ventricular tachycardia characterized by QRS complexes that change directions.

A. R ON T PVC
E. Ventricular Bigeminy
I. Myocardium
M. Atrial Tachycardia
B. Torsades de Pointes
F. Dopamine
J. Right Ventricle
N. Joules
C. SA Node
G. Right Coronary Artery
K. Myocardial Infarction
O. QRS Duration
D. Doppler Ultrasound
H. Thrombolytics
L. Defibrillator
P. P Wave

© 2017 Network4Learning, Inc.

9. *Find the hidden words. The words have been placed horizontally, vertically, or diagonally. When you locate a word, draw a circle around it.*

A	N	P	E	D	L	O	N	G	Q	T	S	Y	N	D	R	O	M	E	Q
L	E	F	T	A	T	R	I	U	M	Y	C	A	T	H	E	T	E	R	W
E	X	F	Q	N	P	A	L	P	I	T	A	T	I	O	N	R	L	N	A
L	L	G	X	Z	T	R	O	P	O	M	Y	O	S	I	N	X	L	K	V
A	N	C	U	K	D	G	Y	S	B	O	X	C	N	N	W	O	H	B	E
P	C	W	V	Z	A	G	Q	A	B	U	N	D	L	E	O	F	H	I	S
P	K	T	I	D	N	S	Q	N	B	B	J	N	B	Q	H	O	Z	T
I	Z	X	O	P	U	L	M	O	N	A	R	Y	A	R	T	E	R	Y	R
T	R	I	C	U	S	P	I	D	V	A	L	V	E	Q	Y	I	I	N	F
L	I	D	O	C	A	I	N	E	A	C	T	I	O	N	O	C	O	T	N
M	Y	O	C	A	R	D	I	A	L	I	N	F	A	R	C	T	I	O	N
W	F	T	D	O	P	P	L	E	R	U	L	T	R	A	S	O	U	N	D

1. At the beginning of contraction, calcium is released and attaches to troponin, allowing cross bridges on the myosin to attach to the actin.
2. An inherited defect of the rhythm of the heart. The QT segment of the heart beat is slightly longer than normal, so the heart takes longer to recharge itself between beats.
3. The first negative deflection following the P wave.
4. Primary pacemaker of the heart. The intrinsic rate of the SA node is 60-100 bpm
5. Vessel that delivers blood from the Left Ventricle to Pulmonary veins.
6. Low pressure chamber that receives oxygenated blood from the pulmonary system via the pulmonary veins.
7. A form of ultrasound that can detect blood flow. Used to diagnose cardiac disease.
8. A thin, flexible tube that is inserted into the heart through a peripheral blood vessel to provide therapy and
9. Conducts impulses from AV node to bundle branches; makes up AV junction
10. The medical term for a heart attack. The blockage or occlusion of a coronary artery causing the loss of blood supply to the heart muscle.
11. Rapid, fluttering heart beats. Heart palpitations can be triggered by exercise, medications, or stress.
12. Rapid, organized atrial contractions that usually result in a heart rate of 250-350 beats per minute. AF is a form of supraventricular tachycardia.
13. Rate; a positive chronotropic effect would result in an increase in rate
14. One-way valve that allow blood flow from Right Atrium to Right Ventricle.
15. Anti-arrhythmic that increases electrical threshold of ventricles during diastole

A. Atrial Flutter
E. Pulmonary Artery
I. Tropomyosin
M. Bundle of His

B. Lidocaine action
F. Catheter
J. SA Node
N. Q wave

C. Myocardial Infarction
G. Tricuspid Valve
K. Doppler Ultrasound
O. Palpitation

D. Chronotropic Effect
H. Long QT Syndrome
L. Left Atrium

© 2017 Network4Learning, Inc.

10.

Find the hidden words. The words have been placed horizontally, vertically, or diagonally. When you locate a word, draw a circle around it.

K	S	K	C	A	R	D	I	O	V	E	R	S	I	O	N	K	X	A	V
M	T	T	O	R	S	A	D	E	S	D	E	P	O	I	N	T	E	S	X
N	R	N	E	N	L	A	R	G	E	D	H	E	A	R	T	M	P	H	A
G	O	X	R	R	V	B	R	F	M	O	B	I	T	Z	I	I	E	J	C
I	K	M	Z	V	L	O	N	G	Q	T	S	Y	N	D	R	O	M	E	U
N	E	T	B	U	P	U	L	M	O	N	A	R	Y	A	R	T	E	R	Y
O	V	I	Y	B	W	L	E	F	T	A	T	R	I	U	M	T	E	S	K
U	O	W	B	I	P	H	A	S	I	C	E	N	E	R	G	Y	Y	Y	O
V	L	Q	C	W	B	D	I	S	U	P	R	E	L	C	E	F	A	V	S
I	U	A	C	L	S	C	O	R	O	N	A	R	Y	S	I	N	U	S	N
C	M	T	F	L	U	T	T	E	R	A	S	Y	S	T	O	L	E	A	S
N	E	P	U	L	M	O	N	A	R	Y	V	A	L	V	E	M	L	X	Y

1. Current from a defibrillator is delivered two ways. Biphasic therapy was introduced in the 1990s and lowers the electrical threshold for successful defibrillation.
2. Amount of blood ejected with each ventricular contraction.
3. Vessel that delivers blood from the Left Ventricle to Pulmonary veins.
4. Venous drainage system of the heart. Returns de-oxygenated blood from the heart to the Right Atrium.
5. An inherited defect of the rhythm of the heart. The QT segment of the heart beat is slightly longer than normal, so the heart takes longer to recharge itself between beats.
6. The medical term for a heart attack. The blockage or occlusion of a coronary artery causing the loss of blood supply to the heart muscle.
7. An unusually large heart. This condition can be a a result of conditions such as an abnormal heart rhythm, stress, or weakening of the heart muscle.
8. One-way valve between low pressure Right Ventricle and low pressure Pulmonary artery. Allows blood flow from Right Ventricle to Pulmonary Artery and prevents blood from flowing back to RV during vent. diastole.
9. A series of advanced treatments for cardiac arrest and other life-threatening conditions.
10. Used for heart block and ventricular arrhythmias. A sympathomimetic that results in pronounced stimulation of beta1 & beta2 receptors of heart and bronchi.
11. A medical procedure by which a trained professional converts an abnormally fast heart rate to a normal rate using defibrillation.
12. A rapid, but organized vibration of the heart muscle. Atrial flutter can result in 250-350 heart beats per minute.
13. Low pressure chamber that receives oxygenated blood from the pulmonary system via the pulmonary veins.
14. Absence of a heartbeat, also known as "flat line". A dire condition in which the heart has no rhythm.
15. polymorphic ventricular tachycardia characterized by QRS complexes that change directions.
16. A heart block where some P waves not conducted through AV node. Some P waves not followed by QRS complexes. P waves that do follow QRS, have consistent intervals.

A. Coronary Sinus
E. Long QT Syndrome
I. Mobitz II
M. Enlarged Heart
B. Pulmonary Valve
F. Isuprel
J. Left Atrium
N. ACLS
C. Myocardial Infarction
G. Pulmonary Artery
K. Torsades de Pointes
O. Stroke Volume
D. Biphasic Energy
H. Cardioversion
L. Flutter
P. Asystole

© 2017 Network4Learning, Inc.

1. *Find the hidden words. The words have been placed horizontally, vertically, or diagonally. When you locate a word, draw a circle around it.*

I	D	A	T	R	I	A	L	T	A	C	H	Y	C	A	R	D	I	A	J
M	A	N	U	A	L	D	E	F	I	B	R	I	L	L	A	T	O	R	O
O	W	Y	G	C	N	P	A	C	E	M	A	K	E	R	X	U	C	P	U
E	K	P	R	I	G	H	T	V	E	N	T	R	I	C	L	E	K	U	L
P	R	O	C	A	I	N	A	M	I	D	E	V	D	I	P	F	M	S	E
G	A	T	R	I	A	L	F	I	B	R	I	L	L	A	T	I	O	N	S
K	F	R	I	G	H	T	A	T	R	I	U	M	T	P	J	X	B	W	B
O	C	R	E	A	R	R	H	Y	T	H	M	I	A	G	Q	H	I	Y	G
O	I	V	T	E	P	I	N	E	P	H	R	I	N	E	L	T	I	Z
B	I	P	H	A	S	I	C	E	N	E	R	G	Y	W	W	H	Z	X	B
V	A	L	S	A	L	V	A	M	A	N	E	U	V	E	R	H	I	C	K
I	L	T	N	M	E	Z	C	A	T	H	E	T	E	R	X	B	U	A	C

1. Current from a defibrillator is delivered two ways. Biphasic therapy was introduced in the 1990s and lowers the electrical threshold for successful defibrillation.
2. An abnormality or irregularity in the heart rhythm.
3. The lower right chamber of the heart that receives deoxygenated blood from the right atrium and pumps it to the lungs through the pulmonary artery.
4. A rapid heart rhythm resulting in 160-190 beats per minute and is a type of supraventricular tachycardia.
5. A measure of electrical energy equal to the work done when a current of one ampere passes through a resistance of one ohm for one second.
6. An implantable medical device that sends electrical signals to the heart to set the heart rhythm.
7. An advanced life support medical device that monitors the heart rhythm and allow the user to manually set the energy delivery and deliver a shock.
8. A heart block where some P waves not conducted through AV node. Some P waves not followed by QRS complexes. P waves that do follow QRS, have consistent intervals.
9. A thin, flexible tube that is inserted into the heart through a peripheral blood vessel to provide therapy and
10. Antiarrhythmic infusion for stable wide QRS Tachycardia. Used to treat life-threatening ventricular tachycardia or symptomatic PVC's.
11. An abnormal, very fast and disorganized heart rate with chaotic electrical activity in the atria of the heart.
12. A forceful attempt at expiration when the airway is closed to stop supraventricular tachycardia.
13. Sympathomimetic that stimulates alpha, beta 1&2 receptors resulting in cardiac stimulation.
14. Low pressure cardiac chamber that receives deoxygenated blood from the systemic venous circulation via the inferior vena cava and the superior vena cava.

A. Joules
E. Atrial Fibrillation
I. Biphasic Energy
M. Procainamide

B. Valsalva Maneuver
F. Mobitz II
J. Epinephrine
N. Catheter

C. Manual Defibrillator
G. Right Ventricle
K. Atrial Tachycardia

D. Right Atrium
H. Pacemaker
L. Arrhythmia

© 2017 Network4Learning, Inc.

2. *Find the hidden words. The words have been placed horizontally, vertically, or diagonally. When you locate a word, draw a circle around it.*

R	I	G	H	T	C	O	R	O	N	A	R	Y	A	R	T	E	R	Y	T
L	D	A	C	L	S	E	O	E	C	A	R	O	N	T	P	V	C	X	X
N	W	T	C	A	R	D	I	O	V	E	R	S	I	O	N	K	Q	N	A
P	D	H	E	A	R	T	M	U	R	M	U	R	N	U	O	T	Y	E	M
O	L	T	K	I	T	R	I	C	U	S	P	I	D	V	A	L	V	E	O
Y	S	N	J	P	P	U	R	K	I	N	J	E	F	I	B	E	R	S	B
C	A	R	D	I	A	C	T	A	M	P	O	N	A	D	E	O	S	S	I
T	S	Y	C	O	R	O	N	A	R	Y	S	I	N	U	S	H	F	N	T
U	O	Z	C	W	R	H	E	A	R	T	R	A	T	E	Y	I	X	M	Z
H	F	R	F	Z	Z	L	E	F	T	V	E	N	T	R	I	C	L	E	U
T	J	P	O	Z	Q	W	A	V	E	V	J	K	F	L	U	T	T	E	R
U	B	E	L	E	C	T	R	O	C	A	R	D	I	O	G	R	A	M	U

1. Venous drainage system of the heart. Returns de-oxygenated blood from the heart to the Right Atrium.
2. The first negative deflection following the P wave.
3. The lower left chamber of the heart that receives oxygenated blood from the left atrium and pumps the blood through the aorta to the body.
4. Coronary artery that delivers blood to the Right Ventricle, AV junction, and the SA node in 55% of the population.
5. A PVC that falls on or very near the T wave.
6. An abnormal "whooshing" sound made by blood flowing through the heart.
7. A test that measures and records the electrical activity in the heart.
8. One-way valve that allow blood flow from Right Atrium to Right Ventricle.
9. A rapid, but organized vibration of the heart muscle. Atrial flutter can result in 250-350 heart beats per minute.
10. A heart block where the PR interval becomes progressively longer until the P wave is not conducted through the ventricle and a QRS complex is dropped.
11. A medical procedure by which a trained professional converts an abnormally fast heart rate to a normal rate using defibrillation.

12. Constriction of the heart that prevent filling of the ventricles. It is usually caused by fluid or blood accumulating in the pericardial sac.
13. The number of complete cycles of the contraction and relaxation of the heart muscle per minute. A normal heart rate for adults is 60 to 100 beats per minute.
14. Final part of the conduction system that initiates vent. depolarization.
15. Continuous monitoring of the electrical activity of a patient's heart with a small, portable ECG machine. The device is typically worn around the neck or waist for a 24-hour period.
16. Low pressure cardiac chamber that receives blood from the Right Atrium and pumps it into the pulmonary artery.
17. A series of advanced treatments for cardiac arrest and other life-threatening conditions.
18. Para-sympatholytic that blocks acetylcholine effects on post cholinergic receptors in smooth muscle and SA-AV nodes.
19. The act of using equipment to send an electrical shock to the heart to stop an irregular heart rhythm. Defibrillation is the only cure to sudden cardiac arrest.

A. Right Coronary Artery
E. Cardiac Tamponade
I. Purkinje Fibers
M. Defibrillation
Q. Heart Murmur

B. Tricuspid Valve
F. Coronary Sinus
J. Electrocardiogram
N. Atropine
R. Left Ventricle

C. R ON T PVC
G. Right Ventricle
K. Mobitz I
O. Cardioversion
S. Holter Monitoring

D. Flutter
H. Q wave
L. Heart Rate
P. ACLS

© 2017 Network4Learning, Inc.

3. *Find the hidden words. The words have been placed horizontally, vertically, or diagonally. When you locate a word, draw a circle around it.*

H	V	K	O	N	I	C	A	R	D	I	O	V	E	R	S	I	O	N	F
D	P	O	M	A	G	N	E	S	I	U	M	S	U	L	F	A	T	E	I
W	C	O	M	M	O	T	I	O	C	O	R	D	I	S	T	J	P	U	A
B	K	W	N	S	T	G	O	O	D	S	A	M	A	R	I	T	A	N	Z
P	R	L	I	D	O	C	A	I	N	E	A	C	T	I	O	N	Q	O	Z
S	I	N	U	S	E	X	I	T	B	L	O	C	K	F	P	H	V	W	Q
S	T	R	O	K	E	V	O	L	U	M	E	M	N	X	T	W	M	C	K
K	K	M	T	R	I	C	U	S	P	I	D	V	A	L	V	E	W	E	J
R	I	G	H	T	C	O	R	O	N	A	R	Y	A	R	T	E	R	Y	A
I	I	K	E	H	S	I	N	U	S	A	R	R	E	S	T	P	B	L	Z
W	R	R	V	A	S	O	V	A	G	A	L	R	E	S	P	O	N	S	E
D	J	Z	B	B	W	S	J	O	U	L	E	S	D	H	D	H	O	K	K

1. A measure of electrical energy equal to the work done when a current of one ampere passes through a resistance of one ohm for one second.
2. A disruption of the heart rhythm caused by a sudden blunt blow to the chest.
3. Anti-arrhythmic that increases electrical threshold of ventricles during diastole
4. Immunity protection provided by each state government and the Federal government to encourage lay responders to treat a victim of sudden cardiac arrest with an AED and CPR.
5. Pause when impulse not conducted out of SA node; pause is exactly 2 R-R intervals.
6. A pause caused by the SA node not firing; pause measures more than 2 R-R intervals.
7. One-way valve that allow blood flow from Right Atrium to Right Ventricle.
8. Caused by stimulation of para-sympathetic Nervous System and results in slowing of the Heart Rate. Can be initiated intentionally with carotid massage or valsalva maneuver.
9. Amount of blood ejected with each ventricular contraction.
10. A medical procedure by which a trained professional converts an abnormally fast heart rate to a normal rate using defibrillation.
11. Coronary artery that delivers blood to the Right Ventricle, AV junction, and the SA node in 55% of the population.
12. Treats Torsades de Pointes, Ventricular Fibrillation. Electrolyte that causes all muscles to contract. Results in depression early after depolarization.
13. The sudden, unexpected loss of the heart function, resulting in the loss of effective blood flow.
14. The act of using equipment to send an electrical shock to the heart to stop an irregular heart rhythm. Defibrillation is the only cure to sudden cardiac arrest.
15. polymorphic ventricular tachycardia characterized by QRS complexes that change directions.

A. Magnesium sulfate
B. Torsades de Pointes
C. Stroke Volume
D. Joules
E. Sudden Cardiac Arrest
F. Sinus Exit Block
G. Vasovagal Response
H. Tricuspid Valve
I. Right Coronary Artery
J. Commotio Cordis
K. Cardioversion
L. Lidocaine action
M. Sinus Arrest
N. Good Samaritan
O. Defibrillation

© 2017 Network4Learning, Inc.

4. *Find the hidden words. The words have been placed horizontally, vertically, or diagonally. When you locate a word, draw a circle around it.*

I	J	C	H	A	I	N		O	F		S	U	R	V	I	V	A	L
P	D	V	B	I	P	H	A	S	I	C	E	N	E	R	G	Y	M	E	Y
X	G	X	Q	P	A	P	B	K	B	Y	X	E	U	Y	A	K	I	K	Z
L	G	T	F	W	D	L	O	N	G	Q	T	S	Y	N	D	R	O	M	E
A	W	T	W	A	E	G	S	V	P	R	I	N	T	E	R	V	A	L	V
B	F	M	E	V	N	M	T	E	L	H	R	S	F	E	Q	W	A	V	E
K	J	Q	M	E	O	S	I	N	U	S	E	X	I	T	B	L	O	C	K
H	Y	G	T	W	S	A	Y	S	I	N	U	S	A	R	R	E	S	T	F
R	I	N	T	R	I	N	S	I	C	R	A	T	E	J	O	U	L	E	S
F	A	W	T	V	N	S	E	P	I	C	A	R	D	I	U	M	G	C	W
Y	I	T	N	R	E	E	Y	H	E	A	R	T	M	U	R	M	U	R	R
V	A	S	O	V	A	G	A	L	R	E	S	P	O	N	S	E	U	O	O

1. An abnormal "whooshing" sound made by blood flowing through the heart.
2. Current from a defibrillator is delivered two ways. Biphasic therapy was introduced in the 1990s and lowers the electrical threshold for successful defibrillation.
3. Used to treat unstable tachy-arrhythmias if regular and monomorphic; Slows atrial conduction through AV node.
4. Caused by stimulation of para-sympathetic Nervous System and results in slowing of the Heart Rate. Can be initiated intentionally with carotid massage or valsalva maneuver.
5. A pause caused by the SA node not firing; pause measures more than 2 R-R intervals.
6. The normal rate for a given pacemaker cells.
7. Measured from where the P-wave starts to where the QRS first leaves the isoelectric line. Represents atrial depolarization and the delay in the AV node.
8. Outer surface of the heart.
9. The first negative deflection following the P wave.
10. An inherited defect of the rhythm of the heart. The QT segment of the heart beat is slightly longer than normal, so the heart takes longer to recharge itself between beats.
11. A measure of electrical energy equal to the work done when a current of one ampere passes through a resistance of one ohm for one second.
12. A four-step process for treating victims of sudden cardiac arrest.
13. Part of the ECG complex that reflects atrial depolarization.
14. Pause when impulse not conducted out of SA node; pause is exactly 2 R-R intervals.
15. Treats Torsades de Pointes, Ventricular Fibrillation. Electrolyte that causes all muscles to contract. Results in depression early after depolarization.
16. An advanced life support medical device that monitors the heart rhythm and allow the user to manually set the energy delivery and deliver a shock.

A. Sinus Arrest
E. PR interval
I. Long QT Syndrome
M. P Wave
B. Epicardium
F. Adenosine
J. Intrinsic Rate
N. Heart Murmur
C. Sinus Exit Block
G. Vasovagal Response
K. Q wave
O. Magnesium sulfate
D. Chain of Survival
H. Biphasic Energy
L. Manual Defibrillator
P. Joules

© 2017 Network4Learning, Inc.

5. *Find the hidden words. The words have been placed horizontally, vertically, or diagonally. When you locate a word, draw a circle around it.*

	C	H	A	I	N		O	F		S	U	R	V	I	V	A	L	A	Q
A	R	R	H	Y	T	H	M	I	A	M	P	A	C	E	M	A	K	E	R
D	J	Y	U	P	C	F	F	F	L	U	T	T	E	R	O	Z	U	N	D
C	P	R	Q	W	A	V	E	P	R	I	N	T	E	R	V	A	L	P	N
W	P	E	R	I	C	A	R	D	I	A	L	E	F	F	U	S	I	O	N
Z	Z	B	O	K	H	S	A	T	R	I	A	L	F	L	U	T	T	E	R
U	G	C	V	C	A	R	D	I	O	V	E	R	S	I	O	N	E	G	J
J	U	N	C	T	I	O	N	A	L	E	S	C	A	P	E	B	E	A	T
R	R	S	I	N	U	S	P	A	U	S	E	P	O	S	J	W	X	Q	A
Q	T	U	U	S	D	L	E	F	T	V	E	N	T	R	I	C	L	E	B
J	D	Y	O	P	Y	B	B	T	R	A	B	E	C	U	L	A	E	W	Q
E	N	N	H	A	Z	E	P	R	O	C	A	I	N	A	M	I	D	E	I

1. Measured from where the P-wave starts to where the QRS first leaves the isoelectric line. Represents atrial depolarization and the delay in the AV node.
2. A four-step process for treating victims of sudden cardiac arrest.
3. cardiopulmonary resuscitation.
4. A rapid, but organized vibration of the heart muscle. Atrial flutter can result in 250-350 heart beats per minute.
5. Rapid, organized atrial contractions that usually result in a heart rate of 250-350 beats per minute. AF is a form of supraventricular tachycardia.
6. Smooth ridges on the walls of the heart.
7. Complex or rhythm that takes over if SA node fails. Beats or rhythm occur after a pause and later than expected.
8. A medical procedure by which a trained professional converts an abnormally fast heart rate to a normal rate using defibrillation.
9. The first negative deflection following the P wave.
10. The lower left chamber of the heart that receives oxygenated blood from the left atrium and pumps the blood through the aorta to the body.
11. An accumulation of fluid in the pericardial sac.
12. An abnormality or irregularity in the heart rhythm.
13. Pause caused by delay in impulse being initiated in the SA node. pause is < 2 R-R intervals.
14. Antiarrhythmic infusion for stable wide QRS Tachycardia. Used to treat life-threatening ventricular tachycardia or symptomatic PVC's.
15. An implantable medical device that sends electrical signals to the heart to set the heart rhythm.
16. Death as a result of sudden cardiac arrest.

A. Sinus Pause
B. Q wave
C. Pericardial Effusion
D. Atrial Flutter
E. Left Ventricle
F. Arrhythmia
G. PR interval
H. Cardioversion
I. Chain of Survival
J. Procainamide
K. Trabeculae
L. Junctional Escape Beat
M. Flutter
N. Sudden Cardiac Death
O. CPR
P. Pacemaker

© 2017 Network4Learning, Inc.

6. *Find the hidden words. The words have been placed horizontally, vertically, or diagonally. When you locate a word, draw a circle around it.*

A	T	R	I	A	L	F	I	B	R	I	L	L	A	T	I	O	N	D	Y
O	W	E	Z	B	I	B	X	R	V	T	R	A	B	E	C	U	L	A	E
N	Y	A	T	R	I	A	L	T	A	C	H	Y	C	A	R	D	I	A	B
C	A	T	O	R	S	A	D	E	S	D	E	P	O	I	N	T	E	S	L
A	H	C	O	M	M	O	T	I	O	C	O	R	D	I	S	V	B	S	O
N	W	S	R	J	D	R	T	Q	P	U	P	L	P	T	F	M	M	Z	Y
M	G	X	D	K	I	O	R	D	R	L	M	V	Z	W	R	J	G	L	K
B	A	L	I	S	E	N	H	H	E	W	X	N	M	A	W	O	Z	B	I
I	V	U	K	C	O	T	A	O	S	Y	R	Y	Q	V	D	G	F	D	V
K	M	N	Q	U	B	P	Q	W	S	N	K	E	R	E	O	X	V	Y	I
A	L	R	Z	Z	M	V	K	U	I	A	R	R	H	Y	T	H	M	I	A
T	N	J	Q	T	R	C	I	I	N	P	R	I	N	T	E	R	V	A	L

1. A disruption of the heart rhythm caused by a sudden blunt blow to the chest.
2. A PVC that falls on or very near the T wave.
3. An abnormal, very fast and disorganized heart rate with chaotic electrical activity in the atria of the heart.
4. Ventricular repolarization; follows the QRS complex.
5. Alternate with epinephrine in patient with pulseless VFib
6. A rapid heart rhythm resulting in 160-190 beats per minute and is a type of supraventricular tachycardia.
7. An abnormality or irregularity in the heart rhythm.
8. polymorphic ventricular tachycardia characterized by QRS complexes that change directions.
9. Rhythms initiated from impulses that originate from the Atrial Ventricular junction. Intrinsic rate 40-60bpm.
10. The amount of blood ejected by the heart in one minute in liters
11. Measured from where the P-wave starts to where the QRS first leaves the isoelectric line. Represents atrial depolarization and the delay in the AV node.
12. Smooth ridges on the walls of the heart.
13. Coronary artery that delivers oxygenated blood to the left side of the heart. Divides into the left anterior descending artery and the circumflex artery.
14. The study of the electrical activity in the heart. Studies and procedures are conducted in the EP Lab of a hospital.

A. Cardiac Output
B. Torsades de Pointes
C. Left Coronary Artery
D. Commotio Cordis
E. R ON T PVC
F. Electrophysiology
G. Vasopressin
H. Junctional Rhythms
I. PR interval
J. Arrhythmia
K. Trabeculae
L. T wave
M. Atrial Fibrillation
N. Atrial Tachycardia

© 2017 Network4Learning, Inc.

7. *Find the hidden words. The words have been placed horizontally, vertically, or diagonally. When you locate a word, draw a circle around it.*

B	E	N	N	S	N	T	E	N	P	D	W	W	J	T	D	R	U	F	U
M	V	L	E	N	D	O	C	A	R	D	I	U	M	A	C	W	B	O	G
F	T	L	I	D	O	C	A	I	N	E	A	C	T	I	O	N	T	W	I
A	M	I	O	D	A	R	O	N	E	N	S	I	L	Q	N	R	M	M	J
A	T	R	I	A	L	T	A	C	H	Y	C	A	R	D	I	A	I	O	X
J	A	B	L	A	T	I	O	N	T	G	T	R	I	G	E	M	I	N	Y
L	E	F	T	V	E	N	T	R	I	C	L	E	Z	Z	L	N	W	F	T
N	K	V	M	P	U	R	K	I	N	J	E	F	I	B	E	R	S	F	X
I	M	U	L	T	I	F	O	C	A	L	P	V	C	V	J	Z	N	W	B
U	A	E	D	G	E	S	C	Z	J	B	R	O	Y	R	U	A	G	U	I
I	M	V	A	S	O	V	A	G	A	L	R	E	S	P	O	N	S	E	I
Z	V	S	T	E	N	T	A	U	A	L	P	D	N	Y	P	K	N	S	L

1. Final part of the conduction system that initiates vent. depolarization.
2. Anti-arrhythmic used to treat atrial-ventricular tachyarrhythmias.
3. Anti-arrhythmic that increases electrical threshold of ventricles during diastole
4. Inner surface of the heart.
5. Premature Ventricular contractions that originate from more than one focus.
6. The lower left chamber of the heart that receives oxygenated blood from the left atrium and pumps the blood through the aorta to the body.
7. Caused by stimulation of para-sympathetic Nervous System and results in slowing of the Heart Rate. Can be initiated intentionally with carotid massage or valsalva maneuver.
8. A tube designed to be implanted in a vessel to help keep it open.
9. A life-saving device that treats sudden cardiac arrest.
10. A technique to remove or render inactive problematic cardiac tissue.
11. Premature ventricular contractions occurring every third beat.
12. A rapid heart rhythm resulting in 160-190 beats per minute and is a type of supraventricular tachycardia.

A. Stent
E. Trigeminy
I. Lidocaine action
B. Multifocal PVC
F. Amiodarone
J. Left Ventricle
C. Endocardium
G. AED
K. Ablation
D. Atrial Tachycardia
H. Purkinje Fibers
L. Vasovagal Response

© 2017 Network4Learning, Inc.

8. *Find the hidden words. The words have been placed horizontally, vertically, or diagonally. When you locate a word, draw a circle around it.*

Q	R	S	D	U	R	A	T	I	O	N	D	O	P	A	M	I	N	E	S
V	A	T	R	I	A	L	T	A	C	H	Y	C	A	R	D	I	A	S	L
W	R	I	G	H	T	C	O	R	O	N	A	R	Y	A	R	T	E	R	Y
D	E	F	I	B	R	I	L	L	A	T	O	R	V	R	V	J	W	W	V
L	W	B	A	B	Q	A	N	B	P	Z	G	J	R	R	K	O	G	N	S
R	O	N	T	P	V	C	Y	O	W	D	C	P	N	Z	P	U	X	P	N
I	Z	D	X	F	M	Y	O	C	A	R	D	I	U	M	A	L	S	B	N
X	Y	J	Z	R	L	M	L	A	V	T	M	O	D	C	Y	E	H	R	J
G	O	B	S	A	N	O	D	E	E	L	S	L	A	T	A	S	C	L	M
R	R	E	D	O	P	P	L	E	R	U	L	T	R	A	S	O	U	N	D
V	E	N	T	R	I	C	U	L	A	R	B	I	G	E	M	I	N	Y	A
V	Z	F	D	L	R	I	G	H	T	V	E	N	T	R	I	C	L	E	E

1. A measure of electrical energy equal to the work done when a current of one ampere passes through a resistance of one ohm for one second.
2. A form of ultrasound that can detect blood flow. Used to diagnose cardiac disease.
3. Primary pacemaker of the heart. The intrinsic rate of the SA node is 60-100 bpm
4. The amount of time it takes for ventricle depolarization. Measured from when the QRS first leaves the isoelectric line to where the ST segment begins.
5. Coronary artery that delivers blood to the Right Ventricle, AV junction, and the SA node in 55% of the population.
6. The lower right chamber of the heart that receives deoxygenated blood from the right atrium and pumps it to the lungs through the pulmonary artery.
7. PVC that occurs with every other beat.
8. A rapid heart rhythm resulting in 160-190 beats per minute and is a type of supraventricular tachycardia.
9. A medical device used to treat a victim with a life-threatening irregular heart rhythm.
10. Sympathomimetic agent that causes peripheral vasoconstriction (alpha effects) and muscle vasodilation (beta effects).
11. Part of the ECG complex that reflects atrial depolarization.
12. Muscle layer of the heart.
13. A PVC that falls on or very near the T wave.
14. A kind of drug that can break up or dissolve clots blocking the flow of blood to the heart muscle. Ideally, the drug should be administered within 90 minutes of being admitted for a heart attack.
15. The medical term for a heart attack. The blockage or occlusion of a coronary artery causing the loss of blood supply to the heart muscle.
16. polymorphic ventricular tachycardia characterized by QRS complexes that change directions.

A. R ON T PVC
B. Torsades de Pointes
C. SA Node
D. Doppler Ultrasound
E. Ventricular Bigeminy
F. Dopamine
G. Right Coronary Artery
H. Thrombolytics
I. Myocardium
J. Right Ventricle
K. Myocardial Infarction
L. Defibrillator
M. Atrial Tachycardia
N. Joules
O. QRS Duration
P. P Wave

© 2017 Network4Learning, Inc.

9. *Find the hidden words. The words have been placed horizontally, vertically, or diagonally. When you locate a word, draw a circle around it.*

A	N	P	E	D	L	O	N	G	Q	T	S	Y	N	D	R	O	M	E	Q
L	E	F	T	A	T	R	I	U	M	Y	C	A	T	H	E	T	E	R	W
E	X	F	Q	N	P	A	L	P	I	T	A	T	I	O	N	R	L	N	A
L	L	G	X	Z	T	R	O	P	O	M	Y	O	S	I	N	X	L	K	V
A	N	C	U	K	D	G	Y	S	B	O	X	C	N	N	W	O	H	B	E
P	C	W	V	Z	A	G	Q	A	B	U	N	D	L	E	O	F	H	I	S
P	K	T	I	D	N	S	Q	N	N	B	B	J	N	B	Q	H	O	Z	T
I	Z	X	O	P	U	L	M	O	N	A	R	Y	A	R	T	E	R	Y	R
T	R	I	C	U	S	P	I	D	V	A	L	V	E	Q	Y	I	I	N	F
L	I	D	O	C	A	I	N	E	A	C	T	I	O	N	O	C	O	T	N
M	Y	O	C	A	R	D	I	A	L	I	N	F	A	R	C	T	I	O	N
W	F	T	D	O	P	P	L	E	R	U	L	T	R	A	S	O	U	N	D

1. At the beginning of contraction, calcium is released and attaches to troponin, allowing cross bridges on the myosin to attach to the actin.
2. An inherited defect of the rhythm of the heart. The QT segment of the heart beat is slightly longer than normal, so the heart takes longer to recharge itself between beats.
3. The first negative deflection following the P wave.
4. Primary pacemaker of the heart. The intrinsic rate of the SA node is 60-100 bpm
5. Vessel that delivers blood from the Left Ventricle to Pulmonary veins.
6. Low pressure chamber that receives oxygenated blood from the pulmonary system via the pulmonary veins.
7. A form of ultrasound that can detect blood flow. Used to diagnose cardiac disease.
8. A thin, flexible tube that is inserted into the heart through a peripheral blood vessel to provide therapy and
9. Conducts impulses from AV node to bundle branches; makes up AV junction
10. The medical term for a heart attack. The blockage or occlusion of a coronary artery causing the loss of blood supply to the heart muscle.
11. Rapid, fluttering heart beats. Heart palpitations can be triggered by exercise, medications, or stress.
12. Rapid, organized atrial contractions that usually result in a heart rate of 250-350 beats per minute. AF is a form of supraventricular tachycardia.
13. Rate; a positive chronotropic effect would result in an increase in rate
14. One-way valve that allow blood flow from Right Atrium to Right Ventricle.
15. Anti-arrhythmic that increases electrical threshold of ventricles during diastole

A. Atrial Flutter
E. Pulmonary Artery
I. Tropomyosin
M. Bundle of His

B. Lidocaine action
F. Catheter
J. SA Node
N. Q wave

C. Myocardial Infarction
G. Tricuspid Valve
K. Doppler Ultrasound
O. Palpitation

D. Chronotropic Effect
H. Long QT Syndrome
L. Left Atrium

© 2017 Network4Learning, Inc.

10. *Find the hidden words. The words have been placed horizontally, vertically, or diagonally. When you locate a word, draw a circle around it.*

K	S	K	C	A	R	D	I	O	V	E	R	S	I	O	N	K	X	A	V
M	T	T	O	R	S	A	D	E	S	D	E	P	O	I	N	T	E	S	X
N	R	N	E	N	L	A	R	G	E	D	H	E	A	R	T	M	P	H	A
G	O	X	R	R	V	B	R	F	M	O	B	I	T	Z	I	I	E	J	C
I	K	M	Z	V	L	O	N	G	Q	T	S	Y	N	D	R	O	M	E	U
N	E	T	B	U	P	U	L	M	O	N	A	R	Y	A	R	T	E	R	Y
O	V	I	Y	B	W	L	E	F	T	A	T	R	I	U	M	T	E	S	K
U	O	W	B	I	P	H	A	S	I	C	E	N	E	R	G	Y	Y	Y	O
V	L	Q	C	W	B	D	I	S	U	P	R	E	L	C	E	F	A	V	S
I	U	A	C	L	S	C	O	R	O	N	A	R	Y	S	I	N	U	S	N
C	M	T	F	L	U	T	T	E	R	A	S	Y	S	T	O	L	E	A	S
N	E	P	U	L	M	O	N	A	R	Y	V	A	L	V	E	M	L	X	Y

1. Current from a defibrillator is delivered two ways. Biphasic therapy was introduced in the 1990s and lowers the electrical threshold for successful defibrillation.
2. Amount of blood ejected with each ventricular contraction.
3. Vessel that delivers blood from the Left Ventricle to Pulmonary veins.
4. Venous drainage system of the heart. Returns de-oxygenated blood from the heart to the Right Atrium.
5. An inherited defect of the rhythm of the heart. The QT segment of the heart beat is slightly longer than normal, so the heart takes longer to recharge itself between beats.
6. The medical term for a heart attack. The blockage or occlusion of a coronary artery causing the loss of blood supply to the heart muscle.
7. An unusually large heart. This condition can be a a result of conditions such as an abnormal heart rhythm, stress, or weakening of the heart muscle.
8. One-way valve between low pressure Right Ventricle and low pressure Pulmonary artery. Allows blood flow from Right Ventricle to Pulmonary Artery and prevents blood from flowing back to RV during vent. diastole.
9. A series of advanced treatments for cardiac arrest and other life-threatening conditions.
10. Used for heart block and ventricular arrhythmias. A sympathomimetic that results in pronounced stimulation of beta1 & beta2 receptors of heart and bronchi.
11. A medical procedure by which a trained professional converts an abnormally fast heart rate to a normal rate using defibrillation.
12. A rapid, but organized vibration of the heart muscle. Atrial flutter can result in 250-350 heart beats per minute.
13. Low pressure chamber that receives oxygenated blood from the pulmonary system via the pulmonary veins.
14. Absence of a heartbeat, also known as "flat line". A dire condition in which the heart has no rhythm.
15. polymorphic ventricular tachycardia characterized by QRS complexes that change directions.
16. A heart block where some P waves not conducted through AV node. Some P waves not followed by QRS complexes. P waves that do follow QRS, have consistent intervals.

A. Coronary Sinus
E. Long QT Syndrome
I. Mobitz II
M. Enlarged Heart

B. Pulmonary Valve
F. Isuprel
J. Left Atrium
N. ACLS

C. Myocardial Infarction
G. Pulmonary Artery
K. Torsades de Pointes
O. Stroke Volume

D. Biphasic Energy
H. Cardioversion
L. Flutter
P. Asystole

© 2017 Network4Learning, Inc.

Glossary

Ablation: A technique to remove or render inactive problematic cardiac tissue.

Adenosine: Used to treat unstable tachy-arrhythmias if regular and monomorphic; Slows atrial conduction through AV node.

ACLS: A series of advanced treatments for cardiac arrest and other life-threatening conditions.

AED: A life-saving device that treats sudden cardiac arrest.

Algorithm: A set of precise rules programmed into a defibrillator to analyze heart rhythms and treat cardiac arrest.

American Heart Association: A non-profit organization that establishes the standards in cardiac care.

Amiodarone: Anti-arrhythmic used to treat atrial-ventricular tachyarrhythmias.

Arrhythmia: An abnormality or irregularity in the heart rhythm.

Asystole: Absence of a heartbeat, also known as "flat line". A dire condition in which the heart has no rhythm.

Atrial Fibrillation: An abnormal, very fast and disorganized heart rate with chaotic electrical activity in the atria of the heart.

Atrial Flutter: Rapid, organized atrial contractions that usually result in a heart rate of 250-350 beats per minute. AF is a form of supraventricular tachycardia.

Atrial Tachycardia: A rapid heart rhythm resulting in 160-190 beats per minute and is a type of supraventricular tachycardia.

Atrium: The upper chamber of each half of the heart.

Atropine: Para-sympatholytic that blocks acetylcholine effects on post cholinergic receptors in smooth muscle and SA-AV nodes.

Basic Life Support: Fundamental treatment provided to a victim to include CPR and AED use.

Beta blocker: Used in stable symptomatic tachycardia that is persistent and does not have a wide QRS.

Biphasic Energy: Current from a defibrillator is delivered two ways. Biphasic therapy was introduced in the 1990s and lowers the electrical threshold for successful defibrillation.

Bradycardia: Slowness of the heart rate, usually less than 60 beats per minute.

Bundle of His: Conducts impulses from AV node to bundle branches; makes up AV junction

Calcium channel blocker: Used in stable symptomatic tachycardias that are persistent and do not have wide QRS-Treatment for Afib., and PSVT.

Cardiac Output: The amount of blood ejected by the heart in one minute in liters

Cardiac Tamponade: Constriction of the heart that prevent filling of the ventricles. It is usually caused by fluid or blood accumulating in the pericardial sac.

Cardiopulmonary Resuscitation: An emergency procedure treating a victim who is unconscious and unresponsive with no signs of circulation.

Cardioversion: A medical procedure by which a trained professional converts an abnormally fast heart rate to a normal rate using defibrillation.

Catheter: A thin, flexible tube that is inserted into the heart through a peripheral blood vessel to provide therapy and

Chain of Survival: A four-step process for treating victims of sudden cardiac arrest.

Chronotropic Effect: Rate; a positive chronotropic effect would result in an increase in rate

Commotio Cordis: A disruption of the heart rhythm caused by a sudden blunt blow to the chest.

Congenital Heart Defect: A birth defect of the heart

Coronary Sinus: Venous drainage system of the heart. Returns de-oxygenated blood from the heart to the Right Atrium.

CPR: Cardiopulmonary resuscitation.

Defibrillation: The act of using equipment to send an electrical shock to the heart to stop an irregular heart rhythm. Defibrillation is the only cure to sudden cardiac arrest.

Defibrillator: A medical device used to treat a victim with a life-threatening irregular heart rhythm.

Dopamine: Sympathomimetic agent that causes peripheral vasoconstriction (alpha effects) and muscle vasodilation (beta effects).

Doppler Ultrasound: A form of ultrasound that can detect blood flow. Used to diagnose cardiac disease.

Electrocardiogram: A test that measures and records the electrical activity in the heart.

Electrophysiology: The study of the electrical activity in the heart. Studies and procedures are conducted in the EP Lab of a hospital.

Emergency medical service: Professional services that respond to 911 calls relating to sudden cardiac arrest.

EMT: A trained and certified professional who can use advanced life support techniques to treat sudden cardiac arrest.

Endocardium: Inner surface of the heart.

Enlarged Heart: An unusually large heart. This condition can be a a result of conditions such as an abnormal heart rhythm, stress, or weakening of the heart muscle.

Epicardium: Outer surface of the heart.

Epinephrine: Sympathomimetic that stimulates alpha, beta 1&2 receptors resulting in cardiac stimulation.

Fibrillation: A rapid twitching of the heart muscles caused by an abnormal and sometimes chaotic discharge of electrical impulses. Atrial fibrillation results in a rapid and irregular heartbeat.

First degree block: Normal Sinus Rhythm with PR interval > 0.20.

Flutter: A rapid, but organized vibration of the heart muscle. Atrial flutter can result in 250-350 heart beats per minute.

Good Samaritan: Immunity protection provided by each state government and the Federal government to encourage lay responders to treat a victim of sudden cardiac arrest with an AED and CPR.

Heart Murmur: An abnormal "whooshing" sound made by blood flowing through the heart.

Heart Rate: The number of complete cycles of the contraction and relaxation of the heart muscle per minute. A normal heart rate for adults is 60 to 100 beats per minute.

Holter Monitoring: Continuous monitoring of the electrical activity of a patient's heart with a small, portable ECG machine. The device is typically worn around the neck or waist for a 24-hour period.

Hypertrophic Cardiomyopathy: A genetic disorder of the heart in which the heart muscle becomes abnormally thick, making it harder to pump blood.

Idioventricular Rhythm: Originates in the ventricle. Rate is 20-40bpm.

Implantable Defibrillator: A medical device that is implanted in the body to diagnose and treat abnormal electrical arrhythmias. If an abnormal arrhythmia is detected, the ICD will apply a shock to restore the heart to a normal rhythm.

Inferior Vena Cava: Large vein that carries deoxygenated blood from the lower venous circulation (below the neck) and empties into the Right Atrium.

Inotropic Effect: Increases force of muscle contraction.

Intraventricular Conduction Defect: A conduction through the ventricles that results in increase time for ventricular depolarization resulting in a prolonged QRS interval > 0.10 in most leads and > 0.12 in all leads.

Intrinsic Rate: The normal rate for a given pacemaker cells.

Isuprel: Used for heart block and ventricular arrhythmias. A sympathomimetic that results in pronounced stimulation of beta1 & beta2 receptors of heart and bronchi.

Joules: A measure of electrical energy equal to the work done when a current of one ampere passes through a resistance of one ohm for one second.

Junctional Escape Beat: Complex or rhythm that takes over if SA node fails. Beats or rhythm occur after a pause and later than expected.

Junctional Rhythms: Rhythms initiated from impulses that originate from the Atrial Ventricular junction. Intrinsic rate 40-60bpm.

Junctional Tachycardia: Junction rhythm with a rate > 100bpm

LAD: Coronary artery that supplies oxygenated blood to the anterior surface of the left ventricle, the ventricular septum, and the papillary muscles of the mitral valve and the bundle of His.

Lead: A wire that conducts electrical current from the defibrillator to the heart. For AEDs, the lead is connected to electrode pads that attach to the patient.

Left Atrium: Low pressure chamber that receives oxygenated blood from the pulmonary system via the pulmonary veins.

Left Atrium: The upper left chamber of the heart that receives oxygenated blood from the lungs and pumps it to the left ventricle.

Left Coronary Artery: Coronary artery that delivers oxygenated blood to the left side of the heart. Divides into the left anterior descending artery and the circumflex artery.

Left Ventricle: High pressure chamber of the heart responsible for pumping oxygenated blood to the systemic circulation.

Left Ventricle: The lower left chamber of the heart that receives oxygenated blood from the left atrium and pumps the blood through the aorta to the body.

Left Ventricular Dysfunction: A condition in which the left ventricle of the heart exhibits decreased functionality. This can lead to heart failure.

Lidocaine action: Anti-arrhythmic that increases electrical threshold of ventricles during diastole

Long QT Syndrome: An inherited defect of the rhythm of the heart. The QT segment of the heart beat is slightly longer than normal, so the heart takes longer to recharge itself between beats.

Magnesium sulfate: Treats Torsades de Pointes, Ventricular Fibrillation. Electrolyte that causes all muscles to contract. Results in depression early after depolarization.

Manual Defibrillator: An advanced life support medical device that monitors the heart rhythm and allow the user to manually set the energy delivery and deliver a shock.

Mitral Valve: One-way valve that allow blood flow from the Left Atrium to the Left Ventricle and prevents blood from flowing back to the LA during Ventricular systole.

Mobitz I: A heart block where the PR interval becomes progressively longer until the P wave is not conducted through the ventricle and a QRS complex is dropped.

Mobitz II: A heart block where some P waves not conducted through AV node. Some P waves not followed by QRS complexes. P waves that do follow QRS, have consistent intervals.

Multifocal Atrial Rhythm: Atrial dysrhythmia; impulse for depolarization originates in 3 or more different foci in the atrium. 3 or more different shaped P waves on ECG.

Multifocal PVC: Premature Ventricular contractions that originate from more than one focus.

Myocardial Infarction: The medical term for a heart attack. The blockage or occlusion of a coronary artery causing the loss of blood supply to the heart muscle.

Myocardium: Muscle layer of the heart.

Normal Sinus Rhythm: A normal heart rate.

P Wave: Part of the ECG complex that reflects atrial depolarization.

Pacemaker: Cells within the heart that can initiate depolarization; external mechanical device that initiates cardiac depolarization.

Pacemaker: An implantable medical device that sends electrical signals to the heart to set the heart rhythm.

Palpitation: Rapid, fluttering heart beats. Heart palpitations can be triggered by exercise, medications, or stress.

Parasympathetic Nervous System: Medulla and mediated by vagus nerve; slows Heart Rate, decreases speed of conduction through AV node, slight depression in contractility.

Paroxysmal Atrial Tachycardia: Atrial tachycardia that starts and stops suddenly.

Pericardial Effusion: An accumulation of fluid in the pericardial sac.

PR interval: Measured from where the P-wave starts to where the QRS first leaves the isoelectric line. Represents atrial depolarization and the delay in the AV node.

Premature Atrial Contraction: An ECG complex that appears earlier than expected; originates from ectopic focus in atrium.

Premature Junctional Contraction: An ECG complex that appears earlier than expected than originates from an ectopic focus in the AV junction.

Premature Ventricular Contraction: An ECG complex that appears earlier than expected that originates from an ectopic focus in the ventricles.

Procainamide: Antiarrhythmic infusion for stable wide QRS Tachycardia. Used to treat life-threatening ventricular tachycardia or symptomatic PVC's.

Pulmonary Artery: Vessel that delivers blood from the Left Ventricle to Pulmonary veins.

Pulmonary Valve: One-way valve between low pressure Right Ventricle and low pressure Pulmonary artery. Allows blood flow from Right Ventricle to Pulmonary Artery and prevents blood from flowing back to RV during vent. diastole.

Purkinje Fibers   Final part of the conduction system that initiates vent. depolarization.

Q wave   The first negative deflection following the P wave.

QRS Duration: The amount of time it takes for ventricle depolarization. Measured from when the QRS first leaves the isoelectric line to where the ST segment begins.

R ON T PVC: A PVC that falls on or very near the T wave.

R wave: The 1st positive deflection following the P wave.

Relative Refractory Period: The time before the cell is fully repolarized when it can respond to a stimulus.

Repolarization: Return of membrane potential to its resting state. K+ move into the cell and Na+ moves out.

Right Atrium: Low pressure cardiac chamber that receives deoxygenated blood from the systemic venous circulation via the inferior vena cava and the superior vena cava.

Right Coronary Artery: Coronary artery that delivers blood to the Right Ventricle, AV junction, and the SA node in 55% of the population.

Right Ventricle: Low pressure cardiac chamber that receives blood from the Right Atrium and pumps it into the pulmonary artery.

Right Ventricle: The lower right chamber of the heart that receives deoxygenated blood from the right atrium and pumps it to the lungs through the pulmonary artery.

SA Node: Primary pacemaker of the heart. The intrinsic rate of the SA node is 60-100 bpm

Sinus Arrest: A pause caused by the SA node not firing; pause measures more than 2 R-R intervals.

Sinus Arrhythmia: Meets criteria for NSR except rhythm is irregular.

Sinus Exit Block: Pause when impulse not conducted out of SA node; pause is exactly 2 R-R intervals.

Sinus Node: A cluster of cells in the upper right atrium that generates electrical impulses and stimulates the heart to contract and pump blood.

Sinus Pause: Pause caused by delay in impulse being initiated in the SA node. pause is < 2 R-R intervals.

Sinus Rhythm: A medical term to describe the normal beating of the heart.

Solatol: Antiarrythmic infusion for stable wide QRS Tachycardia. Depresses heart rate, slows AV conduction, decreases cardiac output, and lowers systolic and diastolic blood pressure.

Stent: A tube designed to be implanted in a vessel to help keep it open.

Stroke Volume: Amount of blood ejected with each ventricular contraction.

Sudden Cardiac Arrest: The sudden, unexpected loss of the heart function, resulting in the loss of effective blood flow.

Sudden Cardiac Death: Death as a result of sudden cardiac arrest.

Supraventricular Tachycardia: Tachycardia with rate > 150bpm; no P waves can be identified.

Supraventricular Tachycardia: A rapid rhythm of the heart, with a pulse of 150-250 beats per minute. The condition can last a few minutes or even days. Treatment may come in the form of cardioversion.

Sympathetic Nervous System: Innervates all parts of the heart and all the blood vessels.

T wave: Ventricular repolarization; follows the QRS complex.

Tachycardia: A rapid heart rate, usually over 100 beats per minute.

Third degree Heart Block: Independent activity of atria and ventricles

Thrombolytics: A kind of drug that can break up or dissolve clots blocking the flow of blood to the heart muscle. Ideally, the drug should be administered within 90 minutes of being admitted for a heart attack.

Torsades de Pointes: Polymorphic ventricular tachycardia characterized by QRS complexes that change directions.

Trabeculae: Smooth ridges on the walls of the heart.

Tricuspid Valve: One-way valve that allow blood flow from Right Atrium to Right Ventricle.

Trigeminy: Premature ventricular contractions occurring every third beat.

Tropomyosin: At the beginning of contraction, calcium is released and attaches to troponin, allowing cross bridges on the myosin to attach to the actin.

Valsalva Maneuver: A forceful attempt at expiration when the airway is closed to stop supraventricular tachycardia.

Vasopressin: Alternate with epinephrine in patient with pulseless Ventricular Fibrillation.

Vasovagal Response: Caused by stimulation of para-sympathetic Nervous System and results in slowing of the Heart Rate. Can be initiated intentionally with carotid massage or valsalva maneuver.

Ventricular Bigeminy: PVC that occurs with every other beat.

Ventricular Fibrillation: Weak disorganized quivering of the ventricle with no identifying QRS complex.

Ventricular Fibrillation: The most common form of sudden cardiac arrest. A sudden, lethal arrhythmia in which chaotic electrical activity results in the ventricles fluttering rapidly and losing the ability to pump blood.

Ventricular Septal Defect: A congenital heart defect where an abnormal opening in the septum separates the ventricles.

Ventricular Tachycardia: Impulse for ventricular contraction originated from ventricle with a rate of > 100pbm.

Ventricular Tachycardia: A fast heart rhythm that originates in the ventricles. Also known as V-tach.

68192428R00083

Made in the USA
Columbia, SC
05 August 2019